THE EARTH SHOOK, THE SKY BURNED

THE
EARTH SHOOK,
THE
SKY BURNED

BY WILLIAM BRONSON

CHRONICLE BOOKS

First Chronicle Books printing April 1986.

Printed in Japan.

Library of Congress Cataloging in Publication Data

Bronson, William.
   The earth shook, the sky burned.

   Reprint. Originally published: Garden City,
N.Y.: Doubleday. 1959.
   Includes index.
   1. Fires — California — San Francisco.
2. Earthquakes — California — San Francisco.
3. San Francisco (Calif.) — History. I. Title.
F869.S357B76   1986   979.4'61   85-31383
ISBN 0-87701-389-6

Cover design: Jorgensen Design, San Francisco

Distributed in Canada by Raincoast Books
112 East 3rd Avenue
Vancouver, B.C.
V5T 1C8

10 9 8 7 6 5 4 3 2

Chronicle Books
San Francisco, CA

CONTENTS

AUTHOR'S NOTES

I WASN'T HERE in 1906, but as a child, a brilliant, blurred image of the San Francisco earthquake and fire was stirred up again and again by my elders until—as with some dreams—it was almost as if I had been. There is nothing extraordinary in my experience. Because the destruction of San Francisco was the biggest event in the lives of most of those who witnessed it, the story is as deeply etched in the memories of my contemporaries' families as it is in mine.

My mother and father were too young to be in school in 1906. All Dad can remember is being hoisted up on someone's shoulder to give him a better view of the burning city at night. The family lived in a shingled house on Monte Vista above Piedmont Avenue in Oakland, and it must have been from there that he saw the bright-as-day sky to the west. He doesn't remember the uphill neighbor's chimney crashing into the house when the shock came, leaving a gaping two-story gash in the south wall, but my grandmother remembered it vividly and told me of the thunderous moment more than once. "It was all very thrilling and dramatic," she wrote in reply to my questioning last spring, "but I'm sure our experience was very ordinary. . . ."

A couple of days after the quake, my grandmother's brother and his wife, accompanied by Jim, their Chinese cook, and five of their "paying guests" arrived from San Francisco for a long stay. Their house, which sat across Van Ness Avenue from St. Mary's Cathedral, had been blown apart by one of the dynamiting teams in the effort to stop the fire's western progress. Counting all—my grandparents; Dad and his seven brothers and sisters; Aunt Mamie, the housekeeper; and the eight refugees from across the Bay—nineteen people lived several months together, cramped but well, in the damaged house and the barn out in back. Jim, the cook, incidentally, saved nothing of his own when the order came to evacuate. But without anyone knowing, he packed a set of china plates he knew were dear to my great-aunt and carried them to Golden Gate Park that night. Nothing else was rescued from the house.

By another selfless act, valuable records belonging to my grandfather were saved from the fire. He had sold his book company in San Francisco a year or so before, but maintained a small office in his successor's quarters in the Phelan Building. Watching the fire across the Bay spread uncontrollably, he assumed his account books—the only record of a considerable amount owed to him—were consumed with the rest of downtown San Francisco. But fortunately, the young man who had bought the business made his way to the offices. Realizing he could save only a trifling few of the dictionaries and encyclopedias in his storerooms, he made a sling from a piece of rope and carted my grandfather's immense ledgers, one under each arm, to safety. Everything he left behind was destroyed later in the day.

Stories of the fire were repeated just as readily on the other side of my family. My mother's recollection is even hazier than my father's, but her father, Bert Hempstead, helped organize and run the camp for Chinese refugees near Lake Merritt. For more than twenty-five years he served as constable in Oakland, and his experience in the camp was the beginning of a long friendship with the people of Oakland's Chinese colony. One of his major jobs was to suppress violence between rival tongs, but their affection for him never waned. I remember a long line of Chinese men standing in the afternoon glare on the day of his funeral in 1937, waiting to take a last look at their friend.

All of this is to point out the kind of recollection that has filtered down through a couple of generations in a very average Bay Area family. Some of the myths surrounding the disaster were mixed in with firsthand accounts, but this, too, is typical.

For every tale I heard while rooting around in search of background material, surely a thousand remain untold. But I have seen the earthquake and fire through the eyes of hundreds who were there, and for the sake of objectivity it may be better that I wasn't there myself. Conflicts in documentation, and there are many, sprang from the fact that a single reporter was physically unable to see more than a tiny part of what transpired, no matter how great his energy.

Like a powerful catalyst, the conflagration quickened the detail of human experience. Simple acts of kindness were framed forever in the City's memory, and myths of impossible proportion which linger to this day grew out of the chaos. Most important, though, the people of San Francisco carried on with the vitality of youth and rebuilt their town in what even today seems an incredibly short time.

In forming this book, I have tried to catch the temper of the day and to record the events which made up the disaster and its aftermath. If it does this, and if it entertains you in the telling, I will have done what I wanted.

ACKNOWLEDGMENTS

I am, of course, indebted to many people for their assistance in the making of this volume. Some lent their aid in the normal routine of their work, and others spent precious hours of their own. All gave their help with great consideration and patience. My sincerest thanks . . .

TO MY FRIENDS for encouragement and valuable criticism: Nada Kovalik, Frances Coleberd, George Burkhardt, Martin Litton, Peter Waller, Clyde Childress, Rozalia De Kanter, Jack Pierce, Steven Johnson, Robert Cowgill, and Dagmar Johnson.

TO OUR FINE LIBRARIES and the librarians whose quiet. competence makes research a pleasure: the library of the California Historical Society, the Stanford University Libraries, the University of California's Bancroft Library and main collection, the Reference Division of the San Jose Public Library, the Palo Alto Public Library, the San Francisco Public Library, the library of the Society of California Pioneers, the Santa Rosa Public Library, and the Oakland Public Library.

TO ROY D. GRAVES, a grand San Franciscan, for his generous work in checking text and captions.

TO MY DEAR GRANDMOTHERS—Mabel Knox Bronson and Mary Jane Hempstead—for their loving help in the early stages.

TO THE PHOTO SOURCES whose files and albums yielded the heart of this book: the California Historical Society, the California Palace of the Legion of Honor, the Bancroft Library, the Bear Photo Service, Edward Zelinsky, the Society of California Pioneers, Mrs. Louise Hilbert, Harry Myers, the Morton-Waters Co., Burton F. Crandall, the San Francisco Chronicle, the San Francisco News, the Oakland Tribune, Mrs. T. T. Tourtillott, Roy D. Graves, the San Jose and Palo Alto Public Libraries, the U. S. Navy, Thomas C. Boyle, Stanford University's Branner Library and Stanford Collection, the San Francisco Chamber of Commerce, Paul Chaumont, and the Automobile Manufacturers Association.

TO THE PHOTOGRAPHERS whose careful work in copying and printing brought the old photos to life: Tom Bogardus, Bear Photo Service, Richard T. Blake, Harvey Willis, the U. C. Library Photographic Service, Morton-Waters Co., Burton F. Crandall, Charles E. Stelling, Moulin Studios, and Keeble & Lohman.

TO THE MEN WHO TOOK THE PICTURES which fill this book. I will be grateful always for the record they left.

TO LAURENCE J. KENNEDY for use of his 1908 M.A. Thesis (U.C., Berkeley) on the progress of the fire.

TO THE FOLLOWING for a miscellany of warm favors: Tanya and Bronson Butler, Chief Rudolph Schubert, Stanleigh Arnold, James de T. Abajian, John Barr Tompkins, Edward F. Braunschweiger III, Charles O'Connor, Rev. Arthur D. Spearman, S.J., George Thompson, Clyde Arbuckle, H. Ross Smith, William Elsner, Jack Plotkin, David Myrick, Rev. Harry B. Scholefield, Rabbi Alvin I. Fine, the San Francisco Examiner, the San Francisco Call Bulletin, the office of the San Francisco Board of Supervisors, Leo S. Levy, Edward O. Scharetg, the Santa Rosa Press Democrat, the California State Bureau of Mines, Edward D. Bronson, Mrs. William Bark, Lillian M. Church, Ruth Scibird, Aubrey Drury, Dr. Edward Tsui, members of the San Francisco Fire Department, Laurence M. Klauber, Ivan S. Rankin, Frank B. Putnam, the U. S. Coast Guard Information Office (S.F.), the Library of Congress, and the U. S. Geological Survey.

TO THE DOUBLEDAY EDITORS who wrestled the book into print: Mary Lou Mueller (now Mrs. Leslie Dorking), who got the thing off the ground, and William Kelley, who brought it home. Special thanks to Art Director Joseph P. Ascherl and Managing Editor Walter Bradbury.

TO PAUL C. JOHNSON and H. LLOYD CHURCHILL, my old mentors, for putting me on this road.

TO KNOX, MEGAN, AND NATHAN, my children, for their understanding patience.

AND TO MY WIFE, MARILYN, without whose criticism, labor, and love I could not have finished this book—although, God knows, there were moments . . .

WILLIAM BRONSON

Palo Alto, California
January, 1959

PROLOGUE: APRIL 17, 1906

View to the east of wholesale district and waterfront from Russian Hill. A smoky haze half obscured the forest of masts; right, Ferry Building, left center, hay schooner, and warships on Bay. Building beyond chimneys, far right, is the Hall of Justice, and coffinlike structure, center, is the Appraiser's Building. (California Historical Society)

SAN FRANCISCO was booming right along with the rest of the nation in spring of 1906. Ten years of increasing prosperity which followed the depression of the mid-1890s had left a vivid mark on the City. Her silhouette was changing, filling out. San Francisco was riding the top of the boom, and optimism colored all levels of city life. It was a lively time for a lively town.

If you had opened the morning paper April 17, you would have read, among other things, that the critics didn't think much of the Metropolitan Opera Company's opening performance at the Grand Opera House the night before, and that Teddy Roosevelt was raising hell again—this time with the insurance trust.

There was nothing new about Roosevelt's crowding the headlines. He had something to say, usually controversial, every day. Only a couple of days before he had blasted away at the muckrakers—those writers who exposed the evils of such diverse institutions as John D. Rockefeller, child labor, and the meat-packing industry. Roosevelt's ire was up because one of the writers attacked Congress in an article titled "The Treason of the Senate."

On the local scene, failure of the Met to come up to expectation was disappointing. The second annual visit

Early photograph of one of San Francisco's most distinguished features—the cable car. Loved now, but only tolerated then, the cable lines crossed the City's hills in a complex pattern in 1906. Picture taken on Clay from Kearny looking west, Portsmouth Plaza on the right. (California Historical Society)

10

South of the Slot was more than the name of a district, it defined a whole segment of San Francisco life. The South of Market boys and girls lived in a crowded cluster of frame houses interspersed with and surrounded by small factories, warehouses, and railroad yards. City Hall dome rises above skyline to the west. (California Historical Society)

of the New York company had been eagerly awaited. More than $100,000 worth of tickets—$10 tops—had been sold in advance, and San Francisco wanted the best. The performance of Carl Goldmark's *Queen of Sheba* unfortunately combined, as one critic put it, ". . . the wrong opera and the wrong singers."

That night, the seventeenth, Enrico Caruso was to sing Don José in Bizet's *Carmen*. The celebrated tenor's appearance was anticipated as the real opening of the season. Madame Olive Fremstad, a Wagnerian soprano, was to take the title role for the first time in her career.

The old Grand Opera House, built in 1876 on Mission between Third and Fourth streets, was one of the few buildings located South of the Slot important to the social life of the City. South of the Slot was the name given then, and still is by some, to the area that

Another nineteenth century snapshot of the City shows Chinese women on shopping expedition along Post near Kearny with Market Street in the background. Rocker-soled shoes worn to emulate high-born, "lily-footed" ladies whose feet were bound in childhood. (California Historical Society)

San Franciscans had an avid interest in fire fighters and fire equipment in the decades between the disastrous fires of the 1850s and the 1906 cataclysm. Here veteran New York firemen parade across Market onto Montgomery Street during a visit in the late 1880s. Palace Hotel in background. (California Historical Society)

Cameraman stood atop a tall building on Post Street between Kearny, right, and Grant to capture this view of the northern section of business district and North Beach, which lies between Telegraph Hill, right, and Nob Hill, left. Grace Church, top left, and the spired California Hotel and Theater were prominent landmarks. Alcatraz Island can be seen dimly in Bay, above North Beach. (Mrs. William E. Hilbert)

Montgomery Street north of Market was and is the "Wall Street of the West." This view was taken in summer of 1905. Intersection of California and Montgomery, center, and Sacramento Street beyond. Fire was to cause severe slump in the stock market and help start the nationwide money panic of 1907. (California Historical Society)

lies south of Market. The Slot was exactly that—a slot in the street between the cable-car tracks which ran a good part of the length of Market Street.

The Market Street cable-car system was itself a subject for discussion that spring. The nine-mile-per-hour cable cars were obsolete, and everyone agreed that they should be replaced. Opposition to unsightly overhead trolley wires and bickering among traction interests had delayed modernization of the transportation system. Considerable support existed for the construction of a subway.

Always in the background, City Hall politicians plied their boodling ways. San Francisco's mayor—handsome, black-bearded Eugene Schmitz—remained popular despite continued potshots at him and his cohort, Boss Abraham Ruef, for the mounting greed of bribe-taking officials under them. No one, even Schmitz' kindest admirers, claimed that city government was cleanly conducted. 'Oiling the skids' had been part of doing business with City Hall for a long time. Even Ruef admitted that his Board of Supervisors, which to everyone's surprise had been swept into office in the November election, was made up of men so hungry for boodle that "they would eat the paint off a house."

If anyone doubted that San Francisco was growing, despite garden-variety corruption, a stroll along Market and the commercial section to the north would have convinced him otherwise. Construction of many large buildings had dramatically marked the passing of one century and the entrance of another.

The Claus Spreckels Building, known to all as the Call Building for the morning paper published there, rose eighteen stories above Market Street at Third to rule the downtown skyline. Other structures, larger, though not so tall—were crowding up to give more substance to San Francisco's claim to metropolitan status. One of these, the James Flood Building at the corner of Market and Powell, had just been completed. At the time, it was the biggest office building in the West.

On the eastern edge of Nob Hill, overlooking the commercial heart of the City, stood a massive white structure—an architectural masterpiece in the tradition of the Greek Revival—the Fairmont Hotel. Below, on Powell Street across from Union Square, a new wing

These three lovely pictures of old Chinatown were taken by one of the world's finest photographers, Arnold Genthe, before fire destroyed the colorful section. (California Palace of the Legion of Honor)

was being added to the St. Francis Hotel, the third of San Francisco's grandest hostelries. The first, then and always of course, was the Palace. Smack up against the clatter and rattle of Market Street, the Palace had been known for decades as the world's finest, and was dear to every Californian.

There were many others. The Ferry Building and the new Post Office, the Mills, Kohl, Chronicle, Merchant's Exchange, Hearst, Crocker, Shreve, and Union Trust buildings, the City Hall, Grace Church, Old St. Mary's, Temple Emanu-El, and the Emporium all had their place against the San Francisco sky. The yet-to-be-completed Monadnock, Newman-Levinson, and Whittell buildings had already staked their claims.

But it wasn't enough just to put up new buildings. San Francisco had been laid out in the early days with little attention to the geography, and the City's growth had followed the original lines. Streets often had to attack the City's dozens of hills from the steepest angles. Many other inconvenient or impractical features were a result of the lack of foresight in pioneer days.

It was serious enough that in 1904, a group of prominent San Francisco men engaged the famous architect, Daniel H. Burnham, to draw up long-range plans for the beautification of the City.

They called themselves "An Association for the Improvement and Adornment of San Francisco." Burnham, who had designed the Chicago World's Fair, labored more than a year and when he finally produced the plans, widespread interest and enthusiasm marked

their acceptance. Times were good, and there was room for extravagant thought.

The plans for a remodeled San Francisco were made on a generous scale. They included new and widened streets, an entirely new civic center, and extension of Golden Gate Park's panhandle across Market and through to the Pacific Mail Lines dock on the bay. Boulevards were to be carved around the City's finest hills—replacing those indifferent streets which crawled blindly straight up and down. All was to be crowned by a great amphitheater cradled on the sides of Twin Peaks overlooking Market Street. But it was an ambitious plan, and no one had yet rushed off to turn the first spade.

As all schoolboys know, San Francisco's eminence began with the Gold Rush of 1849. The City of the Argonauts was built on gold of the Sierras and, later, the silver and gold of the Comstock Lode. Financially, she had dominated the western slope of the continent from the outset. In the twentieth century boom, however, prosperity had come to rest not so much upon the wealth produced in the mines as upon the farms and mills and ranges of the great interior valleys and an explosively growing trade with the Orient. San Francisco was the premier American port of the Pacific. The Panama Canal, already under construction, would further swell San Francisco's port traffic.

America's brief fling at overt colonialism had brought the Philippines into the commonwealth only a few years before. Hawaii, which was closer to San Francisco than New York, was a hub from which Oriental trade fanned. The Boxer Rebellion had been put down in 1900, and since then Secretary of State Hay's Open Door policy had bolstered a mounting trade with China.

Not too many years had passed since that day when Brigadier General Frederick Funston crossed the Palanan River on the island of Luzon to capture the daring leader of the Filipino rebels, Aguinaldo, and thereby end the Insurrection. On April 17, 1906, Funston was at the Presidio, soon to leave for war games in the Pacific Northwest. By chance, he happened to be the ranking army officer in the City. Major General Adolphus Greely, commander of the Pacific Division, was in the East attending the wedding of his daughter.

Chinese and Japanese immigration was an issue in all of California. Traditional resentment on the part of the white majority, particularly among workingmen, carried much weight with politicians, and despite lack of serious trouble or competition from the Orientals, the issue was a live one. America, incidentally, ex-

Sacramento Street starts at Ferry Building, crosses through business district and Chinatown, continues over Nob Hill past the Fairmont Hotel, distant center left, and on to Van Ness Avenue and the Western Addition. This photo, taken in 1905 from Sansome Street, shows the What Cheer House, a famous temperance hotel, left. (California Historical Society)

"The Chutes" on Haight Street near Golden Gate Park. One of three theater-menagerie-fun centers that carried the same name. After the fire, the Chutes Theater held the first public show in San Francisco. (California Historical Society)

Neapolitan fishermen ventured out the Golden Gate at the helms of trustworthy Monterey boats in search of salmon, halibut, crabs. Nets hung to dry from the rail of old Fisherman's Wharf below the foot of Union at the turn of the century. Motors long ago replaced red sails.

Soft, low-grade coal fed the City's furnaces and filled sky with soot when ocean breeze failed. This hazy shot of Market Street was taken from Ferry Building tower in 1898. Horse cars, still in service at time of the quake, used outside tracks while cable cars rode the "Slot." Call Building looms up in the distance. (California Historical Society)

pected one and a half million immigrants from all over the world in 1906.

The subject of public ownership was just as topical. The City's utilities and transportation companies were rumored to depend on the corruptibility of City Hall for favors. The water company, the light company, and United Railways found it much easier to do business by taking care of certain parties in the municipal government. Obviously, the public paid in the long run. Even the powerful Southern Pacific was suspected of "under the table" dealing with Schmitz and his men.

There was plenty of news from other parts of the world that spring for San Franciscans to think and talk about: a revolution in Russia had been crushed by Czar Nicholas—Oklahoma had just been admitted to the Union—suffragettes were arrested for stirring up a fuss at 10 Downing Street in London—the Army tried out the gasoline-driven motorcar ("toys of the rich") and decided to stick with horses and mules—Kaiser Wilhelm, who was lampooned in the American press as "Hot-air Willie," continued to rattle his saber in Europe—the American Bison Society put out the call for money to help in their fight to save the vanishing "buffalo."

You might have read of a mine disaster near Calais, France, that killed 1000 men, or of a very recent earthquake in Formosa which took fifty lives. Calais and Formosa seemed far away from San Francisco, farther by far than today, and the news was easy to forget. Vesuvius, however, was high in the headlines in the week preceding the seventeenth. The classic terror of the Old World was at it again. Ashes rained down on hundreds of square miles of Neapolitan countryside,

16

and lava poured through the streets of small villages on the sides of the volcano. In one large market, 250 persons were killed when the roof collapsed from the weight of accumulated ashes which had fallen from the sky for days. Whole towns were destroyed by this process. Americans took heart, and money was collected and on its way by the seventeenth. Los Angeles had collected and sent $10,000 for Italian relief, but one day later was to divert the money for an even more urgent need. No one in the world could have thought that San Francisco would need more help on the eighteenth than the victims of Vesuvius did on the seventeenth.

By a small, but what was to become a remarkable coincidence, a meeting was held on Tuesday the seventeenth in the courtroom of Judge W. W. Morrow. At this meeting, committees were formed to prepare for future emergencies which might arise in San Francisco. There might have been some question as to just why the committees were needed, but certainly no one objected to this civic-mindedness. San Francisco had one of the finest fire departments in the world and had remained free of conflagration for almost fifty-five years. There hadn't been a killer earthquake since 1868, and, as everyone knew, hurricanes and tornadoes belonged to other parts of the country. A flood was out of the question.

Renowned Palace Hotel, the world's finest for many years, was built around a spectacular covered court. Photo was taken from court's entrance. The interior galleries and bay windows which looked out on Market and Montgomery streets were equally splendid innovations. The spittoon, like the derby, was a standard fixture in 1906. (California Historical Society)

Looking west from the slope of Russian Hill into the Western Addition. The pine-covered Presidio lies against the horizon, projecting into the Golden Gate. Corner of Lombard and Larkin streets in the foreground. 1915 Exposition site beyond tree, right. (California Historical Society)

Painting of Montgomery Street done in 1851 by an unknown artist for the Rothschild Frères, famed European financial house, after the last of San Francisco's disastrous fires in the early days. Rothschild Building, center left, was completely destroyed. (California Historical Society)

In her earliest days, San Francisco had been raked again and again by flames. Six times between December of 1849 and June of 1851 fire destroyed all or a good part of the town, and out of this bitter trial was forged what became one of the most efficient fire-fighting systems of the time. At first, the fire companies were fiercely competitive volunteer groups that vied with each other for the honor of being the fastest, most

Although 1868 earthquake destruction in East Bay cities was more severe than in San Francisco, considerable damage was done in the City, as these photos indicate. This shock is second only to the 1906 disaster in San Francisco's history. Scene, left, in wholesale district: below, at northwest corner of Bush and Market. (Bancroft Library)

modern, most courageous unit in the city. Much of this proud tradition continued after the city assumed direction of the companies in the 1860s.

After the sixth fire, buildings of brick and stone began to go up in the commercial district in place of vulnerable frame structures. Labor was so scarce and expensive in those days that all the brick and stone was shipped in from faraway places—China, Australia, and England. As long as there was gold to be picked up from the stream beds of the Mother Lode, quarrying and brickmaking were not attractive to the workingman. Many of the older buildings downtown were built of stone cut in China. Each stone was dressed and numbered according to the architect's plans, and the final building process involved little more than finding and fitting the pieces together.

The earthquake back in 1868 had been a ripper. Five persons were killed in San Francisco's streets by falling bricks, and severe damage and more deaths were counted across San Francisco Bay in Alameda County —thirty were killed in Hayward and San Leandro alone. There had been fair shakes in 1892 and 1898, too, and every year smaller, but still noticeable quakes were recorded in California. "Nothing to worry about, because there's nothing that can be done about it," was the attitude. "Besides, a good shake is not half so bad as a twister or a hurricane bearing down on you."

There were some who had great concern about the danger of fire. Aside from the brick and stone buildings of the commercial district, including many large "fireproof" structures, the City was made up of frame buildings. Many of the factories and warehouses south of Market were built of brick, but the rooming houses and small homes of workingmen were invariably made of wood. One sixth of the City's population lived South of the Slot. Beyond, small frame buildings lined the blocks which reached into the Mission District and up the hills surrounding it. The Mission District had grown up from the obscure village at the Spanish Mission of St. Francis d'Assisi, better known as Mission Dolores, founded in 1776. Less than sixty years before 1906, the village of Yerba Buena, from which downtown San Francisco was to grow, considered the Mission an inconsequential rural neighborhood.

To the north of the downtown section, Russian and Telegraph hills and the Latin Quarter of North Beach all were built almost entirely of wood. The same was true of the residential district between Powell and Van Ness Avenue which covered the slopes of Nob Hill. Chinatown, which lay on the eastern side of that hill, had been built by Yankees early in the City's develop-

Fifty-two years before the 18-story Call Building burned like a great torch at the corner of Third and Market, this humble predecessor met a similar fate. Building stood at the corner of Clay and Montgomery. (California Historical Society)

Quote from an article entitled "Eastern Impressions of San Francisco" in an eastern newspaper, May 1872: "With the fearful destruction recently wreaked in Chicago by the dread demon of fire vivid in my mind, it is impossible to walk through the streets of San Francisco without feeling a presentiment of an even more terrible fate in store for this great metropolis. One is forced irresistibly to look upon it as a doomed city, and the mind cannot but paint itself a horrible picture of the lapping flames leaping from one frail tinder-box to another, until not one-third of a thriving, prosperous city is swept from existence, but the whole. . . . It needs no gift of prophesy to predict the future, for it is inevitable."

Another of the City's spectacular blazes was brought under control after a difficult fight. A few spectators clambered up Lotta's fountain for a better view of burning Bancroft Building, Third and Market. The year: 1886. (California Historical Society)

Mark Hopkins mansion crowned Nob Hill before Fairmont Hotel was built. Intersection of Pine and Kearny, foreground, Grace Church, center left, Old St. Mary's, at the corner of California and Dupont. Russian Hill on the far right. (California Historical Society)

ment and most of the construction was of brick. In 1906 Chinatown was considered, almost universally, a blight.

Above, several huge, ostentatious mansions, built by fortunes made in the Comstock Lode and the Central Pacific Railroad, shared Nob Hill's prominence with the newly built Fairmont Hotel.

Beyond Van Ness to the west, from Hayes Valley in the south to Cow Hollow in the north, lay the Western

Addition. Perhaps a quarter of the City's homes lay here.

Many of the well-to-do had built in this section, along Broadway, Pacific, Vallejo, Jackson, and Washington and on Van Ness itself. Here too most of the buildings were wooden.

To the west, beyond the densely populated areas, sat Golden Gate Park, already attracting world attention. Hundreds of acres of forsaken sand dunes had been

Burning of Lucky Baldwin's Hotel and Theater at corner of Powell and Market in 1898 took many lives. The three-million uninsured loss broke the swashbuckling Baldwin. (California Historical Society)

Long a convention city, San Francisco bejeweled Market Street for Knights Templar in 1904. Masons and the State Medical Association were in town at time of quake. (California Historical Society)

20

transformed by John McLaren into a garden spot and for years it had served San Francisco as a verdant retreat. In the days which followed April 17, the park would shelter 200,000 homeless San Franciscans beneath its free growing stands of cypress, eucalyptus, and Monterey pine.

In October of 1905, just a bare seven months before, the National Board of Fire Underwriters had declared San Francisco's thirty-six-million-gallon-per-day water system inadequate. After a careful survey, the Board found the hydrant system could not deliver the minimum they felt necessary to guarantee the city safety from major conflagration.

Fire Chief Dennis Sullivan, a veteran of twenty-six years in the department, had battled the supervisors for years to get the money needed to build a supplementary salt-water system and to reactivate dozens of huge, long-neglected cisterns which had been built beneath the downtown streets years before. Because the Fire Department had successfully battled near-disastrous fires in the past with the existing system, indifference had grown up which Chief Sullivan found impossible to overcome. Just seven years before, Lucky Baldwin's sumptuous hotel and theater at the corner of Powell and Market had burned, threatening to take the whole block and perhaps more with it. The Fire Department held that blaze, and many others like it, in check. There would be time to improve the system.

Life was full for San Francisco on the seventeenth. It was a happy, bustling, wonderful time in those "innocent years" and spring weather marked the end of an overcast and rainy winter.

Night approached with the cool breezes from the water that make San Francisco climate a joy.

Before dark, carriages of well-dressed operagoers were on their way to Mission Street. Not everyone in San Francisco was to see Caruso that night, although to read accounts today, it would seem so. Only 3000 of the City's 400,000 heard the tenor. Other thousands, perhaps not so fashionable, were on their way to see Victor Herbert's *Babes in Toyland* at the Columbia Theater on Powell Street, or perhaps to see young John Barrymore in Richard Harding Davis's *The Dictator*.

For those who couldn't afford the Met, the Orpheum offered an evening of vaudeville for as little as ten cents. A dozen other theaters beckoned San Franciscans that night. San Francisco had always demanded first-rate entertainment and plenty of it. The great actress of the late 1800s, Helena Modjeska, uttered her classic appraisal thirty years before:

"If they like you in San Francisco, you're all right."

At the Opera House, Mme. Fremstad failed to stir the critics in her debut as Carmen. Later that night, one of them would write for the next day's paper that she seemed "Dutchy" in the part. Caruso's brilliance, however, overcame the tarnished spots. The pudgy outline of the man on the stage took on heroic proportions when his thrilling voice swelled through the expectant air. San Francisco found another trooper on whom she could heap her unabashed affection. It would have been cruel that night to suggest to those who had been so moved by Caruso that he would not sing in their City again. But he never did.

Wednesday was a working day. The theaters were dark before midnight, and only a few of the City's celebrated restaurants remained open to serve late diners. The streets quieted in the early hours of the morning, April 18.

Two fires, a small one on Market and another at a wire factory out in North Beach, brought clanging fire engines rushing into action. Both blazes were put down without serious difficulty, and weary Chief Sullivan was back in bed by 3 A.M.

The few who looked out over the City in those early, quiet hours later remembered the red and green running lights of ships at anchor in the bay, slowly rising and falling with the gentle swells.

Death and ruin in the wholesale district. (Bancroft Library)

EARTH
IN
AGONY

Clock at Agnew's Insane Asylum stopped at the peak of the earthquake's violence. Death and wreckage at the institution were unmatched anywhere in the earthquake zone. More than a hundred patients and keepers were killed in that terrible moment. The time recorded, 5:13½ A.M., was probably not more than half a minute off. Exact clocks showed the onset to be a few seconds after 5:12 A.M. Tremor built in intensity, paused, then returned with greatest surge of power. Total time: 65 to 75 seconds. (T. T. Tourtillott)

The earth, tortured and twisted by the irresistible force of the earthquake, broke and shifted where filled ground had not completely settled. Although miles from the fault, many of San Francisco's streets were left rippled and torn. (Bear Photo Service)

Five sweet, lonesome peals from the tower bell of Old St. Mary's on California Street in Chinatown rang out to mark the hour. The still, cool air held the promise of another glorious San Francisco day.

The streets were quiet, as they are today at that hour. Here and there a single straggler could be seen trudging his way home—the end of a long night. On Pacific Street, at the foot of Telegraph Hill, you might have heard sounds of music and loud talk from one of the tawdry dance halls that had built the Barbary Coast into a thriving legend.

For others, though, a new day had begun. A few blocks to the southeast of that "sinful" stretch of Pacific Street, men and horses had been at work for several hours in the produce district. Here the sidewalks were piled with sacks of potatoes, onions, turnips, and carrots, all filling the air with an earthy pungence. Old two-, three-, and four-story brick buildings looked down on the busy streets—Front, Davis, Washington, Jackson.

At 5:08 the street lights dimmed and went out. The sun, behind the Berkeley hills to the east, had lightened the sky to a clear blue. A few cable cars and overhead trolleys had already left the car barns to unlimber for the busy hours ahead—harbingers of the clanking herd which, before the sun grew high in the sky, would build the din of another working day.

At 5:12 Police Sergeant Jesse Cook stopped to chat with Al Levy, a young produceman, at the corner of Washington and Davis. The clocks on the tower of the Ferry Building said that it was 5:15—they were running a little fast. But it was to be months before those hands moved any farther, for at that instant, the earthquake struck.

The animals sensed it first: horses shifted and whinnied. Then, with this bare hint, the onrushing violence of a tortured earth broke upon the City to twist and wreck and kill. Jesse Cook, who was later to become police commissioner, remembered hearing a deep rumbling in the distance, "deep and terrible," in his words. And then looking up Washington Street, he actually *saw* the earthquake coming.

"The whole street was undulating. It was as if the waves of the ocean were coming toward me, and billowing as they came."

In the next moment men and animals were to be crushed beneath falling brick walls in the blocks which surrounded the corner at which Cook stood.

The shock lasted little more than a minute, but to a million Californians it seemed an eternity. With a terrifying, wrenching shudder the earth began a crazy dance that toppled towers and chimneys, crumbled rows of simple frame houses to splintered kindling, threw cornices and whole walls into the streets, and twisted steel rails and bridges and pipelines like wet clay.

The first phase of the tremor continued for forty seconds in mounting intensity. Church bells clanged with a senseless fury, and hundreds of thousands thought it was Judgment Day. Those who could find their tongues prayed. Then with seeming deliberation, the shaking ceased for ten seconds, only to return with jarring destruction for another twenty-five seconds. The final violent pulse was followed by small diminishing shudders—idle afterthoughts. During the peak of the fury, the powerful but erratic motion and rhythm reminded one writer of a "terrier shaking a rat." The phrase caught on and remains today the best terse description to be found in the millions of words later written.

The deafening roar produced by the quake was matched only by the violence of the earth's movement. John B. Farish, a mining engineer in town on business and a guest at the St. Francis Hotel, put down his recollections:

"I was awakened by a loud rumbling noise which might be compared to the mixed sounds of a strong wind rushing through a forest and breaking of waves against a cliff. In less time than it takes to tell, a concussion, similar to that caused by the nearby explosion of a huge blast, shook the building to its foundations and then began a series of the liveliest motions imaginable, accompanied by a creaking, grinding, rasping sound, followed by tremendous crashes as the cornices of adjoining buildings and chimneys tottered to the ground."

John Barrymore was also a guest at the St. Francis, but his reaction was never formally recorded. Tradition has it that he was entertaining a young lady—the fiancée of another man—in his suite at the time.

San Franciscans knew they had been through a good one. It wouldn't be far from the truth to say that every soul in San Francisco who could walk—man, woman, and child—was on the street in the minute following the quake.

The silence which followed was almost as awesome as the dreadful sound of the quake. Survivors stood in many places "like speechless idiots," as one observer recalled. When they did talk, the conversation was whispered. In the areas of very severe damage, the trapped and injured cried out in pain and terror, and hurriedly gathered groups struggled to free the victims.

Several people were crushed to death beneath splintered wreckage at Ninth and Brannan streets—a section built over an old creek bed. Fire Department Stables, rear, withstood quake well, but flimsily built frame structures proved lethal. (Branner Library)

Looking like a row of tottering drunks, these houses on Dore Street, south of Market, spewed forth terrified occupants during the moment of the quake. View from Bryant toward Brannan across the undulated pavement which lay above filled creek bed. (Branner Library)

Collapse of the 4-story Valencia Hotel produced one of the greatest single tragedies of the earthquake. The exact number of dead was never certain, since fire swept through before the wreckage could be cleared. Some of the dozens who perished drowned in water from a broken main. The view above was widely published, and accompanying comments told of 30, 45, even 80 persons trapped and killed in the Mission District lodging. (Bear Photo Service)

✗ South of Market, row after row of flimsy frame buildings were tilted or capsized by the shock. Many of the structures were cheap lodging houses and hotels, and it was in this area the greatest toll of lives was taken. The Valencia, Brunswick, Denver, and Cosmopolitan hotels all collapsed and trapped many within the splintered wreckage. ✗

Streets were choked with dust thrown up by falling walls and chimneys. At Larkin and McAllister streets near Market, the huge City Hall was a shambles—$6 million and twenty years of work gone in twenty seconds. With a thunderous roar, walls sheared free and columns toppled into the streets. One of the massive columns smashed against the front of an apartment on Larkin Street and tore the front off it.

Serious damage to buildings in San Francisco occurred in those areas which, over the years, had been filled in and built up with loose dirt. Many blocks in the eastern end of town had once been under the waters of the bay. Montgomery Street was originally the water front, a line which by the time of the earthquake had advanced six blocks to the east. South of Market, old Mission and Willow creeks had been filled in many years before. It was along the course of these streams that dozens of houses, one after another, lurched crazily or collapsed. Along streets in these sections, the pavement bulged up in waves "like a hog wallow," as one newspaper account recorded.

In the wholesale district north of Market, an area which included the produce district, the damage to buildings was also heavy. Here most of the structures were built of brick, and many walls fell to the streets. It was a blessing here, as in the retail district to the west, that both the buildings and the streets were virtually empty. What the death toll might have been if the quake had hit at noon instead of sunrise, no one can guess.

Up on the hilltops, where foundations were anchored in solid rock, and the buildings were built with more care, very little serious damage was done. Practically every chimney was down, of course, and windows, bric-a-brac, china, mirrors, and furniture were destroyed or damaged.

Even in the best built houses on the solidest ground, however, the effects of the quake's intensity were awesome. J. B. Levison, a vice-president of the Fireman's Fund Insurance Company, told in a reminiscence that he had to lunge at the bedroom door in his Jackson Street house two or three times before he finally grasped the knob. Once free, he rushed to put all three of his frightened children in bed with their mother.

Waterfront houses, built over filled ground on shaky foundations, lurched and collapsed when quake struck. (Bear Photo Service)

Steamer on the ways in the Union Iron Works shipyard was knocked off her shoring by the jolt of the quake. (California Historical Society)

Tens of thousands of chimneys crashed through roofs at the moment of the quake, killing many. But some who might have died, like the owner of this bed, were by some lucky chance elsewhere when the quake hit. (Bancroft Library)

"My only thought," he recalled, "was to get the family together so that when the house went down we should all go together."

His house was so badly shaken that water sloshed out onto the bathroom floors from the "reservoirs" above the toilets.

The most terrifying instant for some came when they tried to open the doors to their rooms only to find that the quake had thrown their houses out of plumb just enough to jam all the doors tightly shut.

Down on the water front, the old Long Wharf collapsed under the weight of tens of thousands of tons of Southern Pacific coal. Fortunately, most of the other wharfage, so vital to San Francisco's prosperity, survived. The Ferry Building had been whipped badly by the quake, but still stood straight.

Except in the produce district and the sections of extreme damage south of Market, the dead were scattered at random through the City. A fireman at the Third and Howard Station was killed when he stuck his head out the window during the quake in time to meet a piece of falling cornice. The smokestack at Station C of the San Francisco Gas and Electric Company's yard fell and killed a man. Several were crushed in their beds by falling chimneys—perhaps, we hope, before they awoke to the pitching, rumbling fury of the quake.

The third floor of the fire station on Bush between Grant and Kearny was official residence for Chief Dennis Sullivan. The three-story building sat snug against the California Hotel and housed the men of 2 Engine (Engine Company No. 2) on the first two

28

Key System ferry, Claremont, *toppled in the ways on Alameda's Estuary. If you look closely, you will find a man standing beneath the scaffolding. Imagine the scene if shipwrights had been at work. (Bancroft Library)*

The Mission Station, like other police headquarters, was wrecked in the quake. All stations were either ruined by the tremor or consumed by flames, but luckily, only a few policemen were killed. (Bancroft Library)

floors. At the first movement of the quake, Sullivan was awake and on his feet. Thinking of the safety of his wife, who slept in an adjoining room, he ran for her door. But before he could reach her bedside, a bank of towering smokestacks which had once risen among the turrets of the California Hotel came through the roof of the station. Both Sullivan and his wife were carried by the mass of falling brick through to the first floor. Mrs. Sullivan was injured only slightly, but Sullivan lay unconscious with serious chest and head injuries. He would be missed in the next few days.

San Francisco wasn't alone. A swath twenty to forty miles wide, running 200 miles from Salinas in the south to Fort Bragg in the north, was hit just as hard, or harder in spots. Death and destruction were spread over thousands of square miles.

At Agnew's State Insane Asylum, near San Jose, walls and towers fell in, killing more than one hundred inmates and attendants. Santa Rosa, fifty miles north of the city was a nightmare scene—every brick building in town was down. Oakland, Salinas, San Jose, Fort Bragg, Stanford University, Tomales, Berkeley, Gilroy, Sebastopol—a hundred towns and villages were struck. In that long, horrible minute, hundreds of human lives and hundreds of millions of dollars in property were taken.

Not only were the towns hit by the earthquake's force. The forested hills, the lowlands and mud flats, the valleys of northern California, and even the ocean which beats against the coast were convulsed at the same time.

In the Santa Cruz mountains, fifty miles south of San Francisco, acres of splendid two hundred- and three

Rift passed through the mouth of Alder Creek near Point Arena, leaving a small bridge in shambles. Horizontal displacement at this point was 16 feet. Railroad tracks buckled in the region. (Stanford Collection)

Workmen pose in fissure across from blacksmith's shop on summit above Saratoga. Photo taken an hour after quake. (Branner Library)

Dead horses, as cold and hard as though they might have been chisled from marble, lie in the streets through the morning of the eighteenth, reminding onlookers of the dead humans already carted away. Fires later swept through. (Bancroft Library)

Sonoma Wine Company vaults at Tenth and Howard, eventually consumed by fire. More than 15 million gallons of wine stored in the City were destroyed by quake and fire. (California Historical Society)

All but one of San Francisco's water arteries were broken by the quake. Reservoir mains leading from Crystal Springs Lakes and San Andreas Lake, for which the earthquake fault is named, were wrenched apart or telescoped. (Branner Library)

Thousands of fallen, broken gravestones marked the passing of the quake through cemeteries. Only here, in all the earthquake region, were the sleeping undisturbed. (Branner Library)

hundred-year-old redwoods were whipped into splinters as whole mountainsides slid into sharp valleys below. Along the coast immediately south of San Francisco, 4000 feet of new railroad bed slid down the steep cliff into the ocean.

At the instant of the quake, the crew of the steamer *Argo*, which was plowing through a normal sea about ninety miles north of Point Arena, felt the ship shudder as though it had struck a submerged reef. The vibrations were quick and severe—the captain thought they had struck a raft of logs. Observers on the beaches north of San Francisco noted that the ageless rhythm of the surf was broken. The choppy sea was strangely quiet for a minute.

The editor of San Francisco's *Mining and Scientific Press* awoke in Berkeley "to find the house shaking, amid violent creaking and cracking, so loud as to drown out the crash of falling chimneys. Recognizing that it was an earthquake, one expected it to cease every moment, but after a movement of less violence, the horrible shaking began again, with greater intensity, until it seemed the house must collapse bodily."

In Los Gatos, another writer told of the sound. It was a "deafening . . . rumble and roar like cannonading."

Rural effects were most marked in the area north of Bolinas, through the Tomales region. At Bolinas, build-

ings which sat on piles at the bay's edge were thrown into the water like houses of cards. The same happened on Tomales Bay.

At Point Reyes Station, at the head of Tomales Bay, fireman Andy McNab was stoking up the 5:50 San Francisco commuter's train when the shock came. The first jar rocked the four-car train to the west, and then the return jolt literally knocked the wheels out from under it. The whole train toppled over on its side to the east and lay there like a row of dead elephants. Luckily, no one was injured.

At a nearby farm, milkers were at work in the dairy barn at the time of the quake, and the first shock threw both men and animals to the floor. It would be hours before the cows could be calmed and days before they would give milk again.

All of this happened in less than two minutes. No one in the stricken region had time to notice that the day, April 18, was indeed a beautiful one. In San Francisco later, the sky would be obscured by smoke, but the thought of fire was remote at that early hour.

In most parts of the City, the crowds looked around as the first shock wore off, and the sight of mother and father and the children standing in nightshirts or less brought smiles. With embarrassed hesitation the people of San Francisco began to file back into their homes and apartments.

East on Market Street, late in the morning of April 18. (Bancroft Library)

SKY ON FIRE

No alarms rang, but this company was on its way minutes after the quake. A fine action photo for the time. (California Historical Society)

Flames ate through to Market an hour before tall Call Building, against the smoky backdrop, succumbed. Wall stripped off O'Farrell Street lodging, left. (Bear Photo Service)

EVEN before the jolting shudder of the earth had ceased, fires had kindled in many parts of the City. Days later, Acting Fire Chief Daugherty reported that fifty were started, and it's likely that more were nipped by alert householders. No one can know. In the four days that followed the quake, details of ordinary interest were overwhelmed and lost forever in the immensity of what became the world's greatest conflagration.

Many of the fifty-odd blazes were brought under control by the city's fire companies before the morning had passed. Those that couldn't be checked were eventually to rage across thousands of acres, destroying San Francisco's entire business district and three fifths of her homes and lodgings.

No fire alarms rang that morning. The Fire Department's alarm station, in a small building on Brenham

Place in Chinatown, was a shambles. The alarm system was powered by a series of wet cells which sat in glass jars on long shelves in the station. The quake had toppled them all. Actually, the firemen needed no alarms that morning. As soon as their frightened horses could be caught and calmed, they were hitched to the old steam pumping engines and headed for the nearest sign of smoke.

All public transportation and telephone facilities were useless—victims to the twisting violence of the tremor. Yet tens of thousands of San Franciscans were on the way downtown on foot before the sun was in the sky. With a quake like this one, there would be plenty to see. Many wanted to discover what the shake had done to their stores and offices, factories and warehouses. Thousands of others reported for work, though everyone knew that little business would or could be done. But most were sight-seeing.

In the early hours following the big shock, the greatest fear was of another earthquake. At 5:26 A.M., thirteen minutes after the main shock, the first of many aftershocks rocked the city. Most people had barely regained enough courage to return to their houses, and needless to say, all were quickly back on the streets again.

Those who hiked to high points to look out over the city could see columns of smoke curling into the windless sky from south of Market, the wholesale district near the water front north of Market, and, perhaps, from the isolated fires of the Mission District or Hayes Valley.

General Funston dressed hurriedly after the shock and left his apartment on Washington near Jones for the downtown section. He recalled later having paused at the crest of Nob Hill to survey the scene.

". . . there came not a single sound, no shrieking of whistles, no clanging of bells. The terrific roar of the conflagration, the crash of falling walls, and the dynamite explosions that were to make the next day hideous, had not yet begun."

Farther on down California Street, he found that Grace Church and Old St. Mary's stood without outward signs of damage. Toward Market, smoke was billowing from buildings on both sides of the street.

In spite of the sinister columns of smoke, there was no general alarm in the first hour after the quake. San Franciscans had faith in their fire department.

Four separate fires had sprung up in the business district north of Market, in the area bounded by Sansome and Washington streets. Almost all of the buildings here were brick, and some of the newer ones were rated "fireproof."

35

Quiet crowd fills Market Street in the early morning before troops arrived to make room for fire fighters and authorized workers. Smoke from lower Market area has blotted out the sun. Palace Hotel on right. (Bear Photo Service)

Restless passengers wait in vain for the Valencia Street train. They had yet to learn that the tracks were blocked. (California Historical Society)

More than a dozen fires were burning south of Market—it was here that any fire had a good chance to race out of control. Block after block of flimsy homes and lodging houses were made-to-order tinder.

Small fires at scattered points—Leavenworth and Pacific, Polk near Pine, O'Farrell between Mason and Taylor—were eventually put out, as were the more stubborn blazes at Twenty-second and Mission, and out in Hayes Valley at Buchanan and Golden Gate Avenue.

But at 6 A.M., the City had yet to learn a grim truth—one which would add immeasurably to the distress and destruction of the following days. The story of 38 Engine is typical.

The new firehouse of 38 Engine at the corner of Bush and Taylor had been damaged in the quake, but the men had no trouble getting the horses hitched up and the engine out to the street. The captain went directly to Chief Sullivan's headquarters five blocks away for orders. Sullivan had already been extricated from the debris, but was mortally injured and incapable of directing his men.

The company headed down Market Street toward the farthest column of smoke. The fire had started up in a lodging house known as "Alice's" on Steuart Street a block from the water front, and had spread to a nearby ship's chandlery by the time the firemen arrived.

One of the men threaded a hose onto the hydrant across the street and turned the valve. The men who held the hose braced themselves. But there was no rush of water. The man at the hydrant turned the valve off,

A crowd quickly gathered at this Third and Mission rooming house, attempting to rescue buried occupants. Hundreds dragged from such wreckage were later treated at makeshift hospitals. Scores more died, trapped by the flames. (Bancroft Library)

then on again, but the torrent never came—just a feeble trickle which soon dwindled away.

They tried the hydrant around the corner on Mission, but the story was the same: nothing but an impotent trickle of muddy water. They tried one more hydrant before the suspicion became a forbidding truth: the mains were broken, and there would be no stopping the fire here.

Elsewhere, fire companies found mains that delivered water for a while, but then these too ran dry.

The human toll exacted by the earthquake and fire was by far greatest south of Market Street. It took very few hours for the fires to spread through many blocks here. Heroic groups of firemen and citizens formed to rescue those trapped in fallen buildings, but the unrelenting fires forced one group, then another to fall back and watch crumbled buildings turn into flaming pyres.

A man who had been dragged by rescuers from a lodging house on Folsom Street told of a conversation he could hear between two others who were also trapped in the wreckage. He heard one say,

"I'm not hurt, but there's a beam across my back and I can't get out from under it."

The other answered,

"I'm caught too, it's my wrist. Don't worry, they'll get us out."

Before the splintered timbers that covered them could be cleared away, the fire drove the rescuers into retreat. They could do nothing but stand by helplessly to watch the fire engulf the wreckage, then pass on to leave a smoking drift of ashes.

Among those who were rescued or were able to escape by themselves, many hundreds were in need of immediate aid. The City's hospitals were all damaged, and evacuation was in progress in the early morning. Before the day was over, all the hospitals had removed

Like a wild wind, the fire raced through defenseless frame buildings at Third and Mission streets.

Firemen lift an injured man from the splintered ruins of the Brunswick Hotel on Mission Street.

An abandoned wagon sits in the tracks on Howard, west of Second, awaiting the approaching flames.

Firemen's fight is hopeless as uncontrollable flames sweep over staggered buildings. Water might have been from a sewer, a cistern, or one of the few working hydrants. Arnold Genthe made this dramatic shot. (California Palace of the Legion of Honor)

Early morning view of Post Street, following the earthquake, with Montgomery Street building in background. (California Historical Society)

their patients to safety, and had salvaged a large store of medicines and dressings.

The *Argonaut*, one of San Francisco's pioneer publications, told the story of the Central Hospital in its issue of April 21, printed on a borrowed press in San Jose:

"The first shock demolished the big Central Emergency Hospital and buried the doctors, nurses and patients under a mass of stuff which buckled the beams of the ceilings and smothered those beneath it. Policeman Max Fenner was killed but Policeman Parquetty of the City Hall Station started in and by his own efforts dug out Dr. McGinty, the nurses, and all the patients, including the insane. These he took across the street to the Mechanics Pavilion, where a temporary hospital was immediately installed.

"By six o'clock the wounded were pouring into this hospital. It being the morning when trucks and wagons were just starting out for the day, there were a great number of conveyances ready to carry the wounded immediately away."

38

Policeman leads a dazed and terrified man away from the inferno, Third and Mission. Photo taken from Market. Wracked brick buildings on Main Street await oncoming flames, TOP RIGHT. Fire north of Market, RIGHT, spreads to the west while large crowd gathers across from Battery to watch.
(California Historical Society; Bear Photo Service)

As the fire approaches Market along Fifth Street Wednesday morning, policemen, Army regulars, and bystanders watch calmly, with seeming indifference. Lincoln School at corner. (California Historical Society)

Fire on Howard, near Eighth, burns so fiercely that wires and poles burst into flame. Hundreds of acres South of the Slot burned to the ground during the day Wednesday. (California Historical Society)

Only a day before, the Pavilion had housed a "Skating Masked Carnival," promoted by the secretary of the Board of Supervisors, "Sunny Jim" Coffroth. The Pavilion, a great barnlike arena that covered an entire block across from the City Hall, was known then as the "Madison Square Garden of the West."

The cards were stacked against the City. The firemen faced the impending holocaust not only without water, but without their beloved chief.

Sullivan didn't die for three days. He had first been carried to the Southern Pacific Hospital and then later to the Presidio where he passed on without learning the harsh fate of his City.

San Francisco will never know what might have happened if the stacks of the California Hotel had held. Sullivan was aware, more than any man in the City, of the frightful fire potential that mile after mile of crowded frame houses and shops presented. He had long before laid plans to stop the kind of conflagration that could destroy the City if the water supply somehow should be disrupted. There was water in the bay, and there were ways to pump it into the City. This, plus ruthless, systematic dynamiting and backfiring might have kept the City from going up in smoke. Whether the problem of fighting not one, but fifty fires at scattered points ever occurred to him, no one knows.

Water from the bay did save a good many buildings and most of the wharves along the water front, and dynamite is given much credit for stopping the fire's westward advance at Van Ness Avenue. Without taking accolades from the men who survived to battle the flames, one cannot help but wonder what might have been had Sullivan been able to lead his men.

There was nothing extraordinary about the experience of 38 Engine. In one way or another, each company soon realized that they were almost hopelessly

Broken wall lies in the street across from Union Square on Geary. Mounted troops ride in cable-car tracks amid the horde of casual observers who traveled downtown Wednesday morning. Sun-obscuring smoke rises behind Palace Hotel, center. Whittell Building, steel skeleton on left, and Newman & Levinson Building, above Heine Pianos sign, were half-finished additions to the City's expanding retail district. (California Historical Society)

Arnold Genthe must have known that the elements of a great picture lay before him when he pointed his borrowed 3A Kodak Special down Sacramento and tripped the shutter Wednesday. Called the "Father of Modern Photography," Genthe was an artist of the first rank. This picture has been rated one of the ten best news photos of all time, but his fame rests on a lifetime of distinguished work. Although he left San Francisco after the fire, his enduring portrait of Old Chinatown shall forever bind him to the City. All of Genthe's pre-fire negatives except the Chinatown plates were destroyed Thursday. Will Irwin, who wrote the text of Genthe's Chinatown book, had fortunately urged Genthe to store the plates away from the City, and Genthe left them with a friend in Carmel. The book was published in 1908. Three of the Chinatown pictures are included in the first chapter of this volume. (California Palace of the Legion of Honor)

Dramatic collapse of flats on Golden Gate Avenue near Hyde was a favorite target for photographers. Fire did not reach this section until late Wednesday. In the early part of the day, according to a reliable reporter, a woman sat on the rubble, unmoving, and repeated the question, "No one was killed, but what am I to do?" (Bancroft Library)

handicapped, but the fighting didn't stop when they found the mains dry.

Tens of thousands of gallons of water stood in the sewers, and every main that could be reached with a hose was eventually drained. Twenty-three cisterns holding 16,000 to 100,000 gallons remained in use in 1906. The department fought with whatever it could, and many of the men dropped, literally, from exhaustion before the last flame died.

Some San Franciscans had filled bathtubs and pails with water right after the shock, fearing what was to become a dreadful fact. A few of these little reservoirs saved houses that eventually stood isolated in a sea of smoldering ash. Even wine and vinegar casks were broken open to save a few humble homes in the Italian district on the slopes of Telegraph Hill and in North Beach.

Before 9 A.M. on the eighteenth, the City began to learn what it faced. The almost lighthearted spirit which had prevailed through the crowds at an earlier hour gave way to a sober realization that their beloved San Francisco was burning and there would be trouble stopping it. Fear that the whole town might go didn't come until later in the day, but by mid-morning on Wednesday the eighteenth San Francisco and the world knew that a disaster was in the making.

After the quake, Mayor Schmitz had hurried to the City Hall, and seeing it in ruins, wasted no time in driving downtown to the Hall of Justice on Kearny Street. The Hall, which faced historic Portsmouth Square, was badly damaged. Although the central tower was on the verge of collapse, the Mayor met with waiting police commissioners on the bottom floor, and after surveying what was left of the department, issued his first order. The police were to close every saloon in town. Although many of the outlying stations had been wrecked by the earthquake, most of the six-hundred-man force was ready for duty.

Schmitz and the commissioners drew up a list of fifty prominent names to serve on a "Committee of Safety," and autos were commandeered to carry the message to these well-known men. Ex-mayor James D. Phelan was named chairman.

The committee, working with the Mayor, turned to the problems of greatest need. Besides the injured and dying there were the aged and infirm who needed care. The city faced a battle without food and water, medical supplies, or shelter. Under the cloak of confusion, the criminal element could range at will—looting, robbing, free to molest and destroy. Strict measures had to be taken to prevent criminal anarchy.

One block to the north of his classic Sacramento Street scene, Arnold Genthe paused again to capture a moment of San Francisco's tragedy for the future. In this view, to the east from Clay above Stockton, two young couples half hide a benchload of Chinese children watching the fire beyond Chinatown below. Instead of brocaded finery usually associated with Oriental small fry of the time, these little girls wear voguish picture hats, and the lad reading the newspaper is a ringer for Buster Brown. (California Palace of the Legion of Honor)

Before the second day arrived, the committee's job took on more than an advisory character. It assumed direction of the combined civic and military effort to succor the helpless, maintain order, and fight the fire.

Events began to move quickly. The Mayor dispatched telegrams to Governor Pardee and Mayor Mott of Oakland. His message to Mott was terse.

"Mayor Mott, Oakland
Send Fire engines, hose, also dynamite immediately."

42

Mott needed no explanation—the Oaklanders had only to look across the Bay for the reason.

One of the engines Oakland sent over on the ferry figured in the dramatic stand that saved the Appraiser's Building on Washington Street that same afternoon.

As soon as Governor Pardee got a message from Schmitz, he telegraphed Los Angeles.

"For God's sake send food . . ." was the opening line of his wire.

Los Angeles officials acted with such speed that a trainload of food and medical supplies, along with a group of doctors and nurses, were in San Francisco before midnight of the eighteenth.

General Funston had reached Sansome and California streets before 6 A.M. and found fires burning fiercely and the firemen without water. He quickly realized that troops would be needed, not only to protect federal buildings, but to help the Fire and Police departments. With no way to send a message, Funston tried to flag one of the automobiles "wildly dashing" about, as he put it, but none of the drivers paid any attention to him. He hastened back over Nob Hill on foot, half walking, half running, to the army stables on Pine Street and sent messages to the commanders of Fort Mason, at the foot of Van Ness Avenue, and the Presidio. His instructions were to have all available men march immediately to the Hall of Justice on Kearny Street, where they were to report to Police Chief Dinan. Before he left the downtown area, Funston told the police to find Dinan and inform him of the plan to bring troops in.

After sending the dispatches, he walked back to the crest of Nob Hill and later noted the hushed conversations and lack of excitement in the watching crowds. The day was clear, the breeze imperceptible. Funston went home, left instructions for packing a trunk, drank a cup of coffee, and then left for Army Headquarters in the Phelan Building at O'Farrell and Market. It would be an endless day for the general.

Troops from Fort Mason arrived on Market Street shortly before 7 A.M., carrying rifles with fixed bayonets. By 8 A.M. men from the Presidio had reached the central district. "Cavalry, coast artillery armed and equipped as infantry, field artillerymen mounted on

Refugees huddle in the shelter of the Mint at Fifth and Mission early on the morning of the eighteenth. (California Historical Society)

Men gather aimlessly at the foot of California Street, where a broken main floods wreckage on Market. Fires on either side darken the sky. Choking, eye-burning smoke and the growing heat have thinned the crowd. (Bancroft Library)

Across Market Street tracks, Third Street blazes at the edge of an inferno. Hearst Building, left, has not yet been reached by the dynamiters, and Call Building, right, is just reaching the kindling point. (Bear Photo Service).

Billowing white Ham-and-Eggs Fire shows its vigor as Golden Gate Avenue fire, far left, which firemen battled for hours, dies away. The fresh blaze spread through Hayes Valley and across Van Ness like a prairie fire. The main fires fill the sky with an ominous, mile-long backdrop. Wrecked City Hall, center. (Morton-Waters Company)

A little man stares back into the camera as the innocently started Ham-and-Eggs Fire blossoms forth on Hayes Street. Shortly later, Mayor Schmitz banned indoor cooking indefinitely. (California Historical Society)

their battery horses," made up the force. Almost all of the 1700 troops quartered within the city were downtown by 8 A.M. Police Chief Dinan instructed the first arrivals to patrol Market Street. He was explicit in directing them to shoot anybody caught looting or committing any serious misdemeanor. Funston later wrote that the crowds met his troops with "evident good will."

The Army tug *Slocum* was sent to Fort McDowell on Angel Island, off the shore of Marin County to the north, with orders for the 22nd Infantry to embark, land at the foot of Market, and march to the Phelan Building. Other troops were to be called from Fort Baker in Marin County, Alcatraz Island in San Francisco Bay, Vancouver Barracks across the Columbia River from Portland, Oregon, and the Presidio in Monterey, one hundred miles to the south of San Francisco.

Funston wired Washington to inform the Secretary of War, William Howard Taft, of his actions, and ended his report with the statement,

"I shall expect to receive the necessary authority."

Army regulars were later joined by men from the National Guard, Navy, and Marines, and the Cadet Corps from the University of California at Berkeley.

PROCLAMATION
BY THE MAYOR

The Federal Troops, the members of the Regular Police Force and all Special Police Officers have been authorized by me to KILL any and all persons found engaged in Looting or in the Commission of Any Other Crime.

I have directed all the Gas and Electric Lighting Co.'s not to turn on Gas or Electricity until I order them to do so. You may therefore expect the city to remain in darkness for an indefinite time.

I request all citizens to remain at home from darkness until daylight every night until order is restored.

I WARN all Citizens of the danger of fire from Damaged or Destroyed Chimneys, Broken or Leaking Gas Pipes or Fixtures, or any like cause.

E. E. SCHMITZ, Mayor

Dated, April 18, 1906.

ALTVATER PRINT. MISSION AND 22D STS.

A well-derbied throng, pressed back onto Grant Avenue by the flames on Market, waits, watches, compares notes. (Edward Zelinsky)

All persons without legitimate business were kept away from the fire lines. Many who had motored downtown were ordered into service to chauffeur emergency messengers. Within the city, all communication had to be made in person—on foot, by auto, or horse.

Mayor Schmitz issued his famous proclamation to the city during the morning of the eighteenth.

Many have said the step was unconstitutional, dictatorial. In retrospect, it was, but none protested then.

Buckled rails south of Market rear like ocean waves in front of a man fleeing the intense heat. Some survivors were fortunate to escape with clothes on their backs. (Bear Photo Service)

Firemen stand helpless in front of Slavonian Church, which can be seen in opposite page at the foot of Fell street, ½-inch right of the Ham-and-Eggs Fire. (California Historical Society)

The City might be burning, but it is spring, and young girls have many things to think about. Arnold Genthe made his way to this Russian Hill lookout to catch their fetching smiles. Hall of Justice, Merchants Exchange, and Mills Building dominate the background. (California Palace of the Legion of Honor)

Schmitz' swift action, coupled with the reassuring sight of the military, regular city police, and a thousand volunteer patrolmen, all armed, forestalled any instance of major crime or mass panic. Through the fire and for the long months that followed, strict order was kept in San Francisco.

The Army did not act directly under the orders of either the Police or Fire departments or the mayor. But Funston ordered his officers to consult with the civilian authorities and to comply with their wishes in every way possible. The story is often repeated that San Francisco was under martial law during the crisis, but this is not true. Control remained in the hands of the municipal government.

By midmorning, much of the section south of Market was gone or going. The fires burned through to Market in several places, and thousands watched in fascination as one landmark after another went up. The Emporium, Holbrook, Merrill and Stetson's, and the Hearst Building were gutted. The Grand Opera House and eight carloads of the Met's settings and costumes were consumed.

The fires moved slowly in the wholesale district north of Market, and for a while that morning there was the vain hope that the line might be held at Sansome Street. To the east of Sansome the flames ate slowly through one sturdy brick structure at a time. As flames consumed one building, the temperature built up to the kindling point of the building next door. With each building that burst into flames, the process began again. The scene north of Market was in radical contrast to that in the south where the flames raced through flimsy wooden neighborhoods.

The Fire Department was overwhelmed. Too few men, little water, and a total lack of centralized direction hamstrung their efforts.

If the situation was bad at 9 A.M., it was soon to be confounded on a grand scale. Out in Hayes Valley—that area bounded roughly by Van Ness and Octavia, McAllister and Market—a woman prepared to make breakfast. Her house, a couple of doors west of Gough on Hayes, was undistinguished. It was, a two-story frame structure, much like the others in the neighborhood, and had suffered average damage in the tremor. The chimney was down, a couple of windows were broken, and a mess of broken plaster remained to be cleaned up indoors. The house was still on its foundations and apparently sound otherwise.

Not knowing that her flue had been damaged by the quake, she kindled a fire in the kitchen stove. Sparks set the wall aflame.

46

Since all the fire companies were busy somewhere else, a concerted effort to stop the fire's advance was impossible. The flames crossed Gough to the west, Franklin to the east, Hayes to the south, and were well on their way before noon. This fire, which will always be remembered as the "Ham-and-Eggs" fire, eventually burned over an area larger than that which can be attributed to any of the other fires that started at the time of the quake.

By 1 P.M., the Ham-and-Eggs Fire had burned the St. Nicholas Hotel at Hayes and Market. St. Ignatius Church and College at Van Ness and Hayes, ". . . the finest church of the Jesuit Order in the world," went next, and the fire finally spread to the Mechanics Pavilion. The injured had all been removed from there to makeshift quarters near Golden Gate Park, but the rumor persisted for days that one hundred or more had been trapped and burned to death in the old auditorium.

It was a busy day for every one. Businessmen in the downtown district did what they could that morning to save records and goods. The price of hiring horse, wagon, and driver had jumped fiftyfold between April 17 and 18, but it wasn't lack of money that kept more from being saved. Time ran out too soon. There were not enough hours or wagons.

Alice Eastwood, Curator of Botany for the California Academy of Sciences at the time of the fire, arrived at

Jefferson Square became a refuge for Hayes Valley victims of the Ham-and-Eggs Fire. Young lads examine a well-upholstered car, and nonchalance seems the order of the day. No one in the picture appears to have an interest in the sky full of smoke to the east. (Bear Photo Service)

The flaming Mutual Life Building down California at the intersection of Sansome marks the edge of the north-of-Market fire line. At noon this line extended from Pine to California on Sansome and along Battery from California to the Appraiser's Building on Washington. Engine works away, futilely, in front of the Fireman's Fund office. (California Historical Society)

At midday, the fire blazed along a mile and a half front south of Market and curling, churning columns of smoke and fire rose two miles above the city. The sky burned with a light that cast vague shadows in the day and filled the night with unearthly radiance. It was a brilliant show. Henry Lafler wrote in McClure's Magazine: "All colors and shades were there. Here, for a moment, showed a pale, clear yellow, then again a fiery red. There were perfect blues, there was violet, green, and rose yellow. Then would come dark, sinister, demoniac hues, hateful as hell." (California Historical Society)

This shot was taken from the north side of Market moments after the picture above was snapped from a roof-top near Sutter between Grant and Stockton. Once ignited, the Call Building burned a floor at a time from the top on down. As the temperature reached the kindling point on each floor, the windows burst and the contents were consumed in a rush of fresh air fed through the elevator shafts. Patrolling troops are silhouetted against the smoke from an engine parked at Annie Street between the Palace Hotel and the nearly completed Monadnock Building. (Bancroft Library)

Academy headquarters, on the south side of Market between Fourth and Fifth streets, early that morning. Her only thought was to rescue specimens from the herbarium, up on the sixth floor. This collection of botanical specimens, which had grown under her direction, was considered one of the country's finest. She hailed a young lawyer of her acquaintance to help, and the two climbed the iron railing that had remained more or less intact after the stone staircase within the building had collapsed. Loaded with all the bundles that could be retrieved before the threat of fire drove them away, they were lucky enough to find a wagon for hire and carted the material off to a friend's house on Taylor Street. Later, when the fire approached Russian Hill, they carried the specimens to safety in Fort Mason. The only personal belonging Alice Eastwood saved was the dress she wore. It should be noted that when Miss Eastwood died at the age of ninety-four in 1953, she had been Curator of Botany at the Academy for sixty years.

Tom Crowley, a boatman whose gasoline-driven launches operated out of old Pier 13 at the foot of Vallejo Street, did a turn-away business on the eighteenth and the days that followed. Luckily, he had just received a bargeload of fuel two days before, which made it possible for him to keep his eighteen-boat fleet going steadily. He and his men napped only when they could find a spare hour. They carried thousands across the bay—fifty cents' fare, if you had it—and his waterfront offices served as headquarters for newspapermen who had to reach Oakland to send their stories off. Charles Crocker, head of the Crocker Bank, hired one of Crowley's launches to take heavy boxes and bags of unspecified contents out into the bay and just sit there. Tom Crowley never asked how much they had put aboard—"I didn't want to know," he said.

The Crocker Bank wasn't alone in sending valuables out of the City to safety. Two tellers of the Anglo California Bank carted $1 million in negotiable bonds in a wheelbarrow down Market Street during the morning to the Ferry Building. The bonds, which were not registered and therefore good as greenbacks to anyone who might pick them off the street, were eventually deposited without mishap in an Oakland bank.

Another young man, Amadeo Giannini, packed all the cash and valuable papers from the office of his unpretentious bank at 4 Columbus Avenue into a wagon and drove to his home in San Mateo. Only a few weeks passed before he had opened a new office in the Montgomery Block, and the Bank of Italy was back in business. This bank, later renamed the Bank of America, was to become the world's largest.

Before noon, when the fire lines had become well established, the troops systematically herded the crowds back a block or two to make room for firemen, dynamiters, and messengers. (California Historical Society)

This view down Market was taken a block to the west of the one above as the regulars continued moving the crowd back. Spectators gather at the base of Native Sons Monument while soldiers try to clear the doomed south side. (California Historical Society)

William Keith, the renowned California landscape painter, traveled from his home in Berkeley to see what might be salvaged from his studio. Hundreds of valuable canvases were stored there, the product of many years' work. Unknown to Keith, friends had entered the studio early in the morning and carried out most of his paintings to another repository. Keith never did get to the studio. Flames had engulfed the area around it by the time he reached the City. With nothing else to do, he turned his back on the fire, returned to Berkeley, and began painting a new collection. And the canvases saved by his friends? The fire spread faster and wider than a reasonable man might have foreseen Wednesday morning, and the house to which the paintings had been carried burned to the ground.

Enrico Caruso, the man whose voice had enraptured the Opera House audience the night before, was awakened by falling plaster in his Palace Hotel room. Tradition has it that he ran from the hotel garbed in a nightshirt, with an autographed photo of Teddy Roosevelt under one arm and a towel around his neck, shouting, "Give me Vesuvius!" San Francisco was, in his words ". . . 'ell of a place."

Actually, he was composed enough to walk up to the St. Francis for breakfast. Charlie Olson, broiler cook at the St. Francis, cooked bacon and eggs for the tenor. Apparently the quake hadn't scared Caruso's appetite away. He tipped Charlie $2.50 and cleaned up his plate.

It is not clear whether Caruso spent the first night at Golden Gate Park or the Presidio. His only desire was to leave San Francisco. When the manager finally arranged for a train to leave Oakland, Caruso was on it with the rest of the Metropolitan company. He resolved never to return to the City, and never did.

At noon of the eighteenth the fires that had raged out of control south of Market covered the area from the water front west to Sixth Street, Market south to Folsom. Water pumped from sewers checked the fire at Folsom for several hours.

No. 38 Engine, which had fought up Market Street after its first encounter with the fire on Steuart Street, was in the Call Building at Third and Market by the time 11 A.M. had arrived, hoping to save the landmark. Some of the men were as high as the seventh floor within the building when the fire caught. The intense heat generated by fires all around it turned the towering structure into a furnace. The top floors went first. As the heat reached the critical temperature, windows blew out and the whole floor burst into flame. The fire actually worked down from the top, and by noon the

The smoke-shrouded Call Building and the Palace beyond, with her flag still flying, stand in bright contrast to the gloomy, almost lifeless stretch of Market in front of the gutted Emporium. (Bancroft Library)

Great proportions of the South-of-Market fire, seen from Hopkins mansion, shrivel observers to ant size. The battles to save Mint and Post Office, both behind curtain of smoke, are already underway. (Bear Photo Service)

building stood an empty, ruined shell. The eighteen-story structure was one of San Francisco's monuments to progress, but the elevator shafts through the heart of the structure worked like giant flues to fan the fire. Its burning was a spectacular sight.

50

The 300 emergency patients cared for at the Mechanics Pavilion across from City Hall had to be removed to makeshift quarters near Golden Gate Park in the middle of the day (Wednesday). The rapidly spreading Ham and Eggs Fire threatened to engulf the block-square wooden arena. First patients brought here had been rescued from the ruins of Central Emergency Hospital in the basement of City Hall. Important as the Pavilion was the morning of the eighteenth, this is the only available photo of it taken during those hours. While the world was going to hell downtown, what photographer would bother coming out to shoot this old barn? (Bancroft Library)

Across Market to the north, the Chronicle Building and its spanking new annex were consumed after the fire jumped Sansome Street. With them went the third of the City's major newspapers. The *Daily News,* then a minor paper, was located out on Ninth Street and didn't burn until 4 P.M.

At noon, the northside fires were bound by Sansome from Pine to California, and Battery from California to the Appraiser's Building on Washington. Three fire companies, using cistern water, held this line until the middle of the afternoon.

In the absence of an organized communication system, rumors began to circulate through the City. Some stories told of the fate of the rest of the nation:

"Chicago is under water."

"Seattle and Portland wiped out by tidal wave."

"Los Angeles completely destroyed by quake."

Other reports told of animals swallowed up by cracks in the earth, looters wantonly shot in their tracks by the Federal troops, miscreants hanged in public squares and ghouls found cutting the fingers and ears off corpses for the rings and earrings attached. During the days of the fire there was absolutely no way to confirm or deny such stories. As a result, some of the tales gained such wide currency that they are still believed today, even though investigation has shown them to be wholly untrue.

There were, to be sure, several on-the-spot executions of looters the first day. General Funston later said that only two killings were reported to him, and that

Corner of Geary and Grant looking toward Market Street ruins. Hope that this section, north of the Slot, might be saved persisted until late in the afternoon. (California Historical Society)

those two had been at the hands of the militia rather than the regulars. Newspaper accounts at the time, however, told of twenty to one hundred being shot on the streets for the slightest infraction.

No papers were circulated in the City that day, and the only news San Francisco's 400,000 people received was either by word of mouth or through their own eyes. Right across the bay in Oakland, the *Enquirer's* first

edition told of the Cliff House toppling into the sea. Actually, the Cliff House stood unhurt through earthquake and fire, only to burn a year later.

All during the day, refugees from south of Market and Hayes Valley trudged along the streets leading to Mission Park, Jefferson and Lafayette squares, the Presidio, Golden Gate Park, and the ocean beach. Many stopped at smaller parks and empty lots along the way.

Deep in conversation, strollers turn backs to Mission Street inferno. Corner of Post Office visible, right. (California Historical Society)

Almost everyone carried or dragged or pushed rescued belongings as he went. Some carried bundles in their arms or over their shoulders. Steamer trunks were everywhere to be seen. Crammed full of the pitiful few things a family could save before being driven off by the fire, the trunks were pushed and bullied and cajoled along. ". . . everything with wheels or castors became a wagon," said *Century Magazine*. Baby buggies were piled high. Roller skates were nailed to trunk bottoms. Wheelbarrows, lawn mowers, and sewing machines carried the dishes, pans, pictures, birdcages, rugs, shoes, shirts, skirts, victrolas, tubs, and buckets around which a new home would have to be built. In many a humble family an upright piano was the mark of prosperity. The sight of a sweating, straining breadwinner struggling to push and pull a piano along the sidewalk to safety was not uncommon.

Draymen who the day before charged $1 or $2 for a given job were asking, and getting, $50 and $75 for the same work. Only a few householders could afford this kind of help. In most cases, a person saved nothing more than what he could carry with him. Some of the refugees were lucky to escape with their lives, but even those who were not rushed by the advancing fire could save little more.

The exodus continued in a steady stream through the three days of the fire. Although most people slept out of doors during those nights from fear of a recur-

Portland Telegram, *like other papers over the nation, devoted many whole pages to San Francisco news for days. The world was shocked and fascinated.*

Red Front Store, just west of the Emporium on Market, joins with the Great American Importing Tea Co. to burn hot and bright for a minute, then crumble to earth. (California Historical Society)

North-of-Market fire rages along Montgomery below Telegraph Hill. South of Market, fire blackens the sky. (Bancroft Library)

rence of the earthquake, they had no inclination to give up their homes before the fire arrived. Along the streets that lay in the path of the fires, families sat in front of their houses, waiting. There was no scurrying, no hysteria. Even in the raging south of Market section, relative calm prevailed. The fire might be a block away, but there they sat. Not until the fire was practically upon them would a family finally leave, dragging a trunk or pushing a buggy.

Dynamiting commenced north and south of Market about 1 P.M. on the eighteenth. The Army officer in charge of the operation north of Market, a Lieutenant Briggs, began at the corner of California and Liedsdorff and worked through to Sacramento. The explosion in the first building blew out every window and set it afire. But the squad advanced slowly along Commercial Street to Kearny and along Clay west of Montgomery. Their efforts proved useless.

South of Market, the dynamiting was even more futile. Except for a stand along Eighth Street, no organized line could be drawn. Often the blast would spread rather than hinder the blaze.

A police captain was seriously injured when he went into a saloon at Sixth and Minna streets to investigate a misfire. The charge blew up in his face as he walked in. Later, a Lieutenant Pulis was killed by a premature explosion on Van Ness Avenue.

At times the blasting sounded like an unrelenting artillery battle. It was a matter of amazement to some observers that more were not maimed or killed by explosives. In spite of the fact that little or no good was done by blowing up buildings, dynamiting continued on through the night and next day.

The battle to save the water front started on the morning of the eighteenth and continued unabated until Saturday, the twenty-first. The Navy sent two boats from Mare Island to aid in the fight, the tug *Active* with a detachment of Marines aboard, and the fire boat *Leslie*. Several fire companies worked alongside the sailors and marines on the water front during the day Wednesday, but as the struggle to save the Western Addition shaped up early Thursday, the Navy carried on alone. Marines patrolled the dockside area in the absence of city police.

At 2 P.M. the fire was being held on the north boundary at the Appraiser's warehouse on Washington and Battery. A valiant crew of employees, Marines from the revenue cutter *Bear*, and firemen working an Oakland fire engine struggled under the direction of Appraiser John T. Dare to keep the vulnerable roof from igniting. The Appraiser's Building, the Montgomery Block, and an additional dozen less-distinguished brick structures were to form the only island of buildings that withstood the fire in the downtown area.

The Montgomery Block, the imposing stack of bricks built in 1854 at the foot of Columbus Avenue, admirably defied the fire. With iron shutters and walls many feet thick, the fire couldn't get a foothold. Few buildings had roots as deep in San Francisco history as the "Monkey Block" did. Poppa Coppa's Italian restaurant occupied part of the ground floor and served as headquarters for many serious writers and artists. Gelett Burgess, George Sterling, Will Irwin, Jack London, and many others who gathered there helped to enhance the Block's celebrated name.

Looking down Eddy Street toward Market. Red Front Store, right, has vanished. Fireman in buggy watches last remnant of fire in Emporium Building, while businessman, right, loads records onto wagon. Flood Building, left, burned during night. (Bear Photo Service)

The old United States Mint at the corner of Fifth and Mission and the new Main Post Office up the street at the corner of Seventh were, like the Appraiser's Building, saved by the courage and unflagging labor of devoted employees.

It took seven hours to win the fight at the mint. Water was pumped by hand from basement tanks to wet down the roof and sills and to extinguish small blazes before they had a chance to get a foothold. Frank Leach, superintendent of the mint, Lieutenant Armstrong of the 6th Infantry, and Captain Jack Brady of the Fire Department supervised the defense. Reports at the time mentioned that $40 to $200 million in coin and bullion was stored in the mint's vaults.

One story concerning the mint received wide circulation at the time and, though it had no basis in fact, is sometimes repeated as gospel truth today. It tells of fourteen or more crazed men who stormed the mint to rob its vaults. According to the story, all were shot to death on the steps by the troops on guard.

At the Post Office, the stand against the fire started later in the day and lasted until the sun went down Wednesday night. The earthquake had done considerably more damage to the Post Office than to the other buildings which survived within the fire lines, and the campaign to save it from the flames was as desperate as any fought. Ten employees stayed inside the beleaguered building against the orders of troops and fought with mail sacks dipped in water. Flames

St. Ignatius Church and College, grandest edifice of the Roman Catholic Jesuit Order, stood at Hayes and Van Ness smack in the path of Ham-and-Eggs Fire and was ruined forever—an uninsured loss. Many decades passed before the order fully recovered. (Morton-Waters Company; California Historical Society)

The Daily News, *four years old at the time of the fire, was the only City paper to publish on April eighteenth.* (*San Francisco* News)

South-of-Market fire burned to the waterfront two blocks to the south of Ferry Building, right. (*California Historical Society*)

twice broke into the building through broken windows, but each time the fire was smothered.

The Postal Telegraph office near the corner of Market and Montgomery was a beehive all through the morning and into the afternoon. The telegraph wire which had remained in operation all this time had been San Francisco's only direct link to the outside world. But shortly after the fire crossed Sansome Street at 2 P.M., the office was abandoned. The telegrapher who had worked all those hours sent this final message:

The city practically ruined by fire. It's within half block of us in the same block. The Call building is burned out entirely, the Examiner building just fell in a heap. Fire all around in every direction and way out in residence district. Destruction by earthquake something frightful. The City Hall Dome stripped and only the framework standing. The St. Ignatius Church and College are burned to the ground. The Emporium is gone, entire building, also the Old Flood Building. Lots of new buildings just recently finished are completely destroyed. They are blowing standing buildings that are in the path of flames up with dynamite. No water. It's awful. There is no communication anywhere and entire phone system is busted. I want to get out of here or be blown up.

Chief Operator Postal Telegraph Office
San Francisco, Cal., 2:20 P.M.

By that time, most of Market Street's south side was burning or seriously threatened. At 3 P.M. fire was closing in on the Palace Hotel, ". . . treasured perhaps above everything by San Franciscans."

As the fire spread and filled more and more of the sky with black smoke, thousands of watchers from a dozen high points took heart in the sight of the flag waving gamely from the pole atop the Palace. More than once it seemed to those who watched that the fire must surely have taken the gently waving standard, but the billows would part and show it still safe.

When the flames pressed closely from the back and the side, the bartenders began to pass out bottles of fine liquors and wines to the last to leave. Earlier in the afternoon, when the fire first appeared within striking distance, hard-working employees had drained much of the hotel's internal supply to wet down the roof and other vulnerable points. The gallant try will always be remembered in admiration, but when the fire companies arrived they found that the water on which they had counted had disappeared. Their chance to save the proud old hotel was gone with it. It is problematical whether the Palace could have been saved, even with water, by the time the Fire Department arrived. At 3:30 P.M. the smoke cleared momentarily, and the flag could no longer be seen. By that time the hotel itself had been given up to the flames. "Bonanza Inn," as Oscar Lewis lovingly dubbed her, was gone before the sun went down.

Southward, the fire crossed Folsom and burned to Harrison. There it joined another blaze and by 4 P.M. the flames took all that remained east of Eighth and south of Folsom to Harrison.

Back on the other side of Market, the tempo began to pick up. The flames had not swept from block to block with the frenzy that had marked the fire south of Market, but temperatures were generated so great that stone withered and crumbled. "Marble and brick and concrete blocks fell in on themselves or, in the wake . . . of fire, glowed into heaps of lime and brick and ash and wire-draped junk."

Sight-seers who milled through Union Square in the early morning give way to apprehensive refugees. (Edward Zelinsky)

The Ham-and-Eggs Fire spread across debris-choked Larkin Street to the shattered City Hall, and then slowly ate through the City's records in the following days. Earthquake damage was severe along this stretch of Larkin. (California Historical Society)

At 2 P.M., the west side of what is now called the Embarcadero—then called East Street—was afire from the Ferry Building to Pacific Street, but the area north and west of Washington and Battery was safe.

Earlier, before the flames had advanced to the corner of Davis and Jackson streets, thousands of chickens were humanely released from freight cars pulled up on a siding next to the Swift and Company packing house. Pursuing children from Telegraph Hill pressed in on them from one side and the inferno from the other.

Late in the afternoon, when an aftershock threatened to collapse the half-ruined Hall of Justice, the Committee of Safety moved headquarters first to Portsmouth Square across the street, and then up Nob Hill to the newly built Fairmont Hotel. The fire, which approached from the south and east, reached the Hall an hour after the committee adjourned.

Portsmouth Square had been a center of activity all day. Prisoners of the city jail in the Hall of Justice had been as terrified at the time of the quake as anyone else in the City, but unlike others, they had nowhere to go. The prisoners, and corpses from the morgue in the same building, were taken to the historic square early in the day. "Desperate" prisoners were eventually taken in manacles to the Federal prison on Alcatraz Island, and unfortunate drunks and petty criminals who had found themselves "inside" that morning were herded by the National Guard to Fort Mason.

Corpses gathered by the Coroner's office were piled in Portsmouth Square together with bodies from the morgue. In the afternoon, as the fire approached, the bodies were hastily buried in shallow graves, and then abandoned at 5 P.M. when the heat drove back every living thing in its path.

The Hall of Justice was burning by then. Before the police left the area there had been time to cover sal-

Injured man is helped from auto to bed at improvised hospital in Golden Gate Park after trip from Mechanics Pavilion. On this strip along Stanyan Street, private homes were opened and tents were pitched for care of patients. (Edward Zelinsky)

A coatless man (center, right) beckons frantically on Mission Street, looking west from Third. (Bancroft Library)

vaged records with damp blankets to protect them from the raging heat which was to circle the square.

This homely patch of land, Portsmouth Square, which sits today in surroundings not much different from those which were there before, had seen the City grow from a village. For the first time since its beginning, not a soul touched a foot upon the square, or for that matter, stood within blocks of it all the night through.

The fire that jumped Sansome followed the path of the dynamiters west to Kearny. For a while, the firemen thought the westward march of the flames might be stopped there. The demolition crew, still determined to stop the fire, loaded up a drug store at the corner of Clay and Kearney. Having run out of dynamite, they used the only explosive available—black powder. When the charge was set off, bedding from an upstairs room was set aflame by the blast and sent hurtling across Kearney. Chinatown was doomed. Before midnight, almost 10,000 Chinese had left the dozen blocks that made up San Francisco's most famous district and joined the parade of the homeless.

Louise Herrick Wall wrote in *Century Magazine* that the small feet of the Number One wife of a Chinese merchant tottered on three-inch soles ". . . for the first time in broad day beside her lord, like a fearless American."

The retail district west of Kearny and south of Bush still had not been touched by the fire. During the day, the firemen had been successful in keeping the flames from crossing Market, and they stubbornly fought along Kearny south of Clay. But at 9 P.M. the fire crossed Kearny at Bush and continued westward.

The crowds had retreated before the advancing fire and by nightfall the downtown section was largely deserted.

An anxious companion watches first aid given at Golden Gate Park (Bear Photo Service)

National Guardsman poses with bayonet fixed on Kearny Street late in the afternoon. Fire has moved up from the wholesale district and jumped the street in its westbound march between Sacramento and Clay. (California Historical Society)

There was hope the Palace might be saved, even after the Call Building burned. Her flag cheered observers on the hills through the morning and early afternoon. (California Historical Society)

James B. Stetson, a Gold Rush veteran who at a grizzled seventy years of age still directed the California Street Railway Company, wrote that at 8 P.M.,

"Very few people were on the streets. Goldberg, Bowen & Co. were loading goods into wagons from their store on Sutter, between Grant and Kearny. I attempted to go in to speak to the salesman, with whom I was acquainted, but was harshly driven away, by an officious policeman, as if I were endeavoring to steal something." Stetson's indignation was not an isolated reaction to the stern attitude of Funston's troops and the police.

A little later that night a group of weary soldiers started a small fire in Delmonico's Restaurant on O'Farrell—or was it the Alcazar Theater next door? The record grows dim in certain details—merely to brew some coffee to brace them on their patrol. But this comforting fire somehow went out of control. This fire and the one that crossed Kearny at Bush burned relentlessly through the retail district that bounded Union Square on the east. By midnight most of the retail district and Chinatown were in ashes. Powell Street became the new rallying point.

Once darkness had fallen, hundreds of thousands of watchers saw a sky as bright as day along a forty-block front. Light filled the sky for miles around. People in Sonoma and Santa Clara counties, fifty miles to the north and south, can remember a sky so luminous that ". . . you could read a newspaper at midnight."

Looking from Oakland and Berkeley, observers saw great black clouds of smoke tinged with pink from the billowing flames. An occasional blast of explosive gave the picture ". . . a suggestion of warfare," in the words of one writer.

On the south side of town, the fire that had raced eastward from Eighth Street back to Second between Folsom and Harrison moved southward and reached the sheds of the Southern Pacific Railroad at Townsend Street. At 10 P.M., the Fire Department and a handful of Navy men managed to keep the vulnerable roofs damp through the threatening period. The water was pumped from a narrow channel extending in from the bay three blocks south of the sheds. The Southern Pa-

National Guardsmen back an engine to the curb in front of the Palace as firemen prepare to defend the historic inn. By this time, the few civilians still within the fire lines are leaving, and but a handful of police, soldiers, and firemen remain behind. Three-lamp street lights, like the one behind the fireman's head, were used along Market Street and Van Ness Avenue before the fire. (Bear Photo Service)

At 3:30 P.M. the Palace flag is gone—burned to an ash by the blistering smoke which poured up from the heart of the lovely old lady. The picture on the upper right shows the Grand Hotel, left, and the Palace, abandoned to the fury of the flames. Blocks away, Arnold Genthe rested his camera on the sill of a window in his Sutter Street apartment and shot the white billow rising from the burning Palace beyond the spire of the First Congregational Church and the St. Francis Hotel, right. Everything within his lens would be gone by sunrise. (Bear Photo Service; California Historical Society; California Palace of the Legion of Honor)

With the Palace gone, all the south side of Market was left to burn. A couple of solitary figures, the blurred image of an auto on an urgent errand, abandoned belongings, and weak, lengthening shadows fill the big street in this late afternoon view taken from Jones Street looking east. (California Historical Society)

The fire rages savagely at the corner of Eighth and Market beyond a pathetic pile of abandoned household goods. (California Historical Society)

cific terminus was to become a center of greatest importance in the weeks following the fire.

As soon as the danger passed at the depot, the fire fighters moved westward to save other buildings along the street. Townsend became part of the southern boundary of the City's burned area.

After nightfall, the Ham-and-Eggs Fire had spread from the Mechanics Pavilion to the ruined City Hall, where it slowly ate through room after room, taking with it a good part of the City's records. It took the fire three days to finish the job.

On the west side, the Ham-and-Eggs Fire was stopped before dawn of the nineteenth, and it was done by sheer persistence on the part of the firemen. There were no vacant lots or hills to help, and the wind never gave the men an advantage. Holding the fire along Octavia Street and Golden Gate Avenue, as they did, should be remembered as one of the fine achievements of the department during the fire.

On the south, the Ham-and-Eggs Fire crossed Market at Ninth and reached Twelfth by midnight. Here it joined the fire advancing from South of the Slot to begin a massive thrust into the Mission District. At mid-night the line of the fire was halfway around the bend made by each of the streets between Harrison and Mission as they enter the Mission.

Jack London had rushed down to the City from his place in Sonoma County to cover the biggest story of a lifetime. Later, he wrote in *Current Literature,*

". . . remarkable as it may seem, Wednesday night, while the whole city crashed and roared into ruin, was a quiet night. There were no crowds. There was no shouting and yelling. There was no hysteria, no disorder. I passed Wednesday night in the path of the advancing flames, and in all those terrible hours, I saw not one woman who wept, not one man who was excited, not one person who was in the slightest degree panic-stricken . . . Never, in all San Francisco's history, were her people so kind and courteous as on this night of terror."

Not twenty hours had passed since the big quake, but already most of the business district, all of the area south of Market, Chinatown, and Hayes Valley were, for practical purposes, destroyed. One hundred thousand people were homeless. And the fire still had two and a half days to burn.

The fire swept through the South of Market section like a scythe. Cavalrymen pause before Roman ruins toward the foot of Market Street, left. Above, from what was Kentucky Street and is now the extension of Third, a rare late-afternoon view into the South of Market fire from the south. Below, a group of refugees who paused in the smoking ruins. Note the makeshift wheelbarrow, left center, and the man in front of the chiffonier, right, who raises his glass in a friendly toast to the cameraman. (California Historical Society; Stanford University Library; Morton-Waters Company)

Late Wednesday, long after the South of Market had been surrendered, the defenders turned their hoses to the north side. In a scene of hopelessness strides a lonely figure, head bent away from the heat. In a day, Market Street would be jammed as it was early Wednesday morning, but on Thursday homeless refugees, not sight-seers, would throng the broad avenue. (Bear Photo Service)

Arnold Genthe waited for horsemen to ride into range before he shot toward the flames burning at the rear of buildings on the north side of Market. Of the fire, a writer in Over-land Monthly said, ". . . it followed the ground, it scaled the heights, it burned through steel and rock and licked up wood as though it were straw."
(California Historical Society)

Black hulk of the National Brewery on Fulton Street glowers down upon a hurrying wagonload of refugees. Wrecked City Hall dome looms above the smoke. All of this was leveled before the sun went down. (California Historical Society)

64

THE LONG DAY: APRIL 19-21

Refugees stream down Market toward the Ferry Building. (Bancroft Library)

Early Thursday morning, light from fire on the east side of Nob Hill, left, and the combined Ham-and-Eggs and South-of-Market fire, right, reflects off waters of the Golden Gate. Photo taken from the old St. Francis Yacht Club in Sausalito. The trail of the fire extended more than four miles by this time. (California Historical Society)

One solution to the problem of transportation. Original caption read: "Anything to get out of town." (California Historical Society)

POWELL Street, which stretches up and over Nob Hill then down to North Beach, had by Wednesday night become a rallying point, as had Kearny and Sansome before it. It was a "natural" line along which the fire fighters could make an effective stand. For several hours it looked as though the fire north of Market might be stopped there. The fires of the wholesale and financial districts, which had merged and burned westward in one front earlier in the day, met the Delmonico fire at Geary late in the evening and the two, together, raged on the east side of Powell in an almost continuous line from Eddy on up to Washington, above Chinatown.

The huge Flood Building, at the corner of Market and Powell, still withstood the flames. Union Square, a block-square island of green lawns and trees between

Geary and Post, was lighted by the glare from the inferno which roiled on three sides. Only the St. Francis
Hotel, which loomed up a dozen stories across Powell
from the square, was not on fire by midnight.

It was the expanse of Union Square, along with the
scattered vacant lots on Powell above the Square, that
led the fire fighters to think they might hold the line
here. On the west side of the street at the top of Nob
Hill sat both the Leland Stanford mansion and the
Fairmont Hotel—and both were fortunately far back
from the street.

With a thin stream of water drawn from an old
cistern, the firemen held the line for more than two
hours. Eighteen hours of labor in killing heat had left
most of the men exhausted, but with little equipment
and less water at their disposal, they continued the
battle.

It was perhaps inevitable that the fire should jump
Powell, as it had the earlier barriers. At 3 A.M., or there-
abouts, the wooden spire of a small church near Bush
Street caught a flying ember, and the frail, dry building
became a torch. That was all it took. Powell Street was
abandoned as a fire line, and Van Ness Avenue, the
wide boulevard eight blocks to the west, became the
City's last hope.

In the hours between the break-through at Powell
and dawn, a determined fight was made to save the
old Mark Hopkins mansion which, until the building
of the Fairmont, had dominated San Francisco's skyline. Years before, the building had been given to the
University of California to be used as an art school and
gallery. The Hopkins Institute of Art, as it was known,
stood like an old palace, crowned with stacks and gables,
turrets and dormers, and a tasteful profusion of filigree
—an archtype of Victorian architecture.

Many students and teachers, including a detachment
sent by President Benjamin Ide Wheeler from the
University at Berkeley, had worked to save the Institute's famous art collection during the day. Hundreds
of canvases and statues were carted out during the day
Wednesday, but as the fire approached during the
night, much had to be abandoned. Some of the paintings taken from the building were left on the lawn of
the Flood mansion—the sturdy brownstone which stood
catercorner across California—only to be consumed
later.

The flames, which ate along Bush and Pine streets
from the break-through point on Powell, turned up
Mason and eventually jumped to the western wing of
the Institute. The first of four mansions built by the
Central Pacific's "Big Four"—Hopkins, Stanford,

*Thursday's papers carried headlines like this, recounting
on-the-spot executions of looters, and for several days,
stories of crime and swift justice, or injustice, were printed.*

*Jefferson Square took on a slightly more permanent look
the second day. Families staked out small claims, and
tents made from anything available—rugs, blankets, tar-
paulins—were thrown up. The scene was repeated in
dozens of other similar places—Golden Gate Park, Lafayette Square, Mission Park, and the Presidio, to name a
few. You might have heard piano music and singing
voices, had you been here the night before. Someone produced a bottle of whisky, and before the evening was done,
two young ladies sat on the piano, glasses in hand, and
sang "There'll Be a Hot Time in the Old Town Tonight."
(Bancroft Library)*

These two views of the fire approaching from the east were taken 50 feet apart in Lafayette Square, but by different photographers on different days. The upper shot was taken Wednesday morning while the South of Market burned. The lower view was taken as the fire descended the western slope of Nob Hill Thursday. Same houses can be seen, right.
(California Historical Society; Bancroft Library)

Headline may have been partially accurate, but generally the soldiers drove civilians back from fire lines.

"We then played a stream on the Mark Hopkins Institute and surrounding buildings until the water supply in that cistern under the pavement at California and Mason streets was exhausted. I then put 3 Engine to work on the cistern inside the grounds of the Institute. While working there we were visited by His Honor the Mayor, who came up into the building to encourage us in our good work, and left orders to work our best in trying to save the Institute. Under the direction of Battalion Chief O'Brien, we continued working until the fire surrounded us in a very threatening manner, and to save our apparatus we had to leave there."

By daybreak, nothing was left of Mark Hopkins's monument to his own success, or of Leland Stanford's counterpart next door.

The flames had crossed California Street between Mason and Taylor to claim the Flood, Huntington, and Crocker mansions, and then circled back to the east along Sacramento. The Fairmont, in its glacial beauty, was still untouched. But the same breeze which helped hold back the fire from the south earlier, gently

Huntington, and Crocker—blazed like a giant firebrand in the night. The Stanford house, which shared the block with the Hopkins estate, was next to go. The other two, farther west on Nob Hill, survived until after sunup. The captain of 3 Engine, who fought in the struggle to save the Institute, remembered this of the incident later:

Tens of thousands tramped to the foot of Market Street to cross the Bay Thursday. Smoke still rose from ashes. (Bancroft Library)

Thousands turned to the west for safety. Bits of the human stream that flowed out Lombard Street to the Presidio were caught in these two photos. Wheelbarrows, carts, and shank's mare carried the homeless and their belongings. (Edward Zelinsky)

blew the searing heat off Sacramento Street until the windows could no longer resist. The flames entered a northwest corner room where paints and varnishes were stored. Before the morning was over, what had been fittingly called "the most magnificent pile of marble in the world" was gutted.

All this while the Ham-and-Eggs Fire continued to blaze, and as the crew of volunteers and firemen struggled to bring it under control on the west, the eastern boundary continued to expand.

At dawn on Thursday, only two fire fronts remained. One was proceeding through the Mission, leaving the South of Market District devastated in its wake. That fire had been joined by the southern arm of the Ham-and-Eggs Fire, which had jumped Market. The other

71

Commanding view of the fire in the Mission was taken from the Sixteenth Street Hill Thursday afternoon. The fire burned out the Mission in a straight, broad sweep to Twentieth Street before it was stopped. Fire's boundary nearest camera is Dolores Street. Westerly breezes helped hold this arm of the fire in check. Upper Market Street cuts diagonally across from center left to lower right. The boulevard, center, leading into the burning section is Sixteenth Street. (Bear Photo Service)

Washington Square crowded with refugees from Latin Quarter. (Edward Zelinsky)

front fanned out north, west, and south from Nob Hill, with Washington Street the northern boundary.

Toward Market Street, the Delmonico fire, having joined with the north of Market fires to jump Powell, met with the eastern arm of the Ham-and-Eggs Fire advancing between Market and Geary.

By that time, Chinatown was gone, as was the neighborhood of frame buildings that lies in the saddle between Nob and Russian hills. To the east, the fire slowly ate through the brick district leading from downtown toward Telegraph Hill.

That morning, clouds of smoke lay over the City to a height of two miles. The incredible flames of Wednesday, estimated by some as mile-high, were gone. Market Street, where flames had towered into the sky the day before, was a forsaken path along which a steady, hurried stream of refugees poured toward the Ferry Building.

From the East Bay, the sight in the early morning was magnificent. Sunlight struck the uppermost billows of the thick masses of smoke and set them ablaze.

During the day of Thursday, the nineteenth, the fire ate its way down the western face of Nob and Russian hills toward Van Ness. Details blend and blur in the memories of most of those who were close to the fire

BELOW LEFT: *Young militiamen pose at the intersection of Post, Montgomery, and Market streets. Masonic Temple, left. (Bancroft Library)*

72

This close-up of the fire as it came down Nob Hill Thursday was made by Arnold Genthe. Note men on haunches, left. (California Palace of the Legion of Honor)

lines then, but everyone in the city knew that Van Ness was to be the battle line.

News of the outside world was not to be had in San Francisco, and the rest of the world had just as much trouble finding out what had happened and what was expected to happen in the burning town. The Boston *Evening Transcript* reported April 19 that ". . . very little connected information was received this morning." Many papers printed a false report that the fire was under control. One Chicago editor heard that the City was on fire and ordered his writers to, ". . . burn the whole town down!" Much imagination went into the day's record.

As a matter of side interest, it was on the nineteenth that Pierre Curie, codiscoverer of radium, was run over and killed by a horse and wagon in Paris. Could anyone who might have read the small item, crowded onto a back page that Thursday, have imagined the dead man would later be regarded as one of the founders of a new age?

Of more immediate importance was the news that Admiral Goodrich had landed with the Pacific Squadron and hundreds of marines and sailors to help fight the fire and patrol the streets. The fleet had been standing offshore near San Diego 500 miles to the south when news came Wednesday that San Francisco was burning.

Another Naval expedition was dispatched on Thursday. A small boat left Mare Island Naval Shipyard

To the east from Alta Plaza Thursday night. The same scene viewed from Berkeley evoked this description ". . . flames rose to the high heaven and glowing clouds pierced the starlit sky; the sight was one of desolating splendor." (California Historical Society)

near Vallejo carrying a three-man demolition team. These men were to systematically blow up block after block of houses along the east side of Van Ness Avenue as the fire advanced to the west. The plan was to level a block-wide strip with dynamite and then to set backfires which would burn to the east and meet the oncoming north-of-Market front.

The fire in the Mission District continued to burn along an irregular front all through the day and into the night of the nineteenth. The flames were fought stubbornly all the way, and the east and west boundaries—Howard and Dolores—were held largely through sheer tenacity of the fire fighters. This arm of the fire was finally stopped early Friday morning along Twentieth and Twenty-first with water from an old cistern on a hill above the fire line. For a moment the firemen were stymied when they found their exhausted horses couldn't pull the engines up the slope. But as the *Chronicle* told the story later, bystanders manned the ropes and the ". . . engines were taken with a rush and hurrah up the steep grade of Dolores . . . to make the impressive stand which, with the dynamiting of the north side of Twentieth Street, resulted in checking the fire along that line."

The dramatic battle shaping up on the north of Market, however, was the center of attention. It was a long day of preparation and waiting. While the fire raged, the municipal government and the military worked at high pitch.

Much has been said about the conduct of the Army during the fire. No one statement can adequately sum up the multitude of opinions which were voiced when it was all over. Some were filled with praise, even adulation; others were scornful. There is little doubt that the Army did much good. But the soldiers, acting on the orders of their superiors, also did irreparable harm, indirectly, by ordering hundreds of unwilling homeowners from their property long before any earthly good could possibly come of it. In most cases, a few more hours would have meant the saving of some personal property instead of none. Others were forced

Looking north from above Market Street near Buchanan. Smoke rises from Van Ness, Russian Hill, and North Beach. Fairmont Hotel and Nob Hill are outlined against the sky. Protestant orphanage lies beyond the tents. (Bear Photo Service)

away from their homes even though they were prepared to fight to the last to save them. Those who were willing to fight along with the firemen were almost universally turned away from the fire lines by the soldiers. Perhaps in the long run, it would have made no difference. In all likelihood the fire would have run much the same course no matter what happened.

One specific instance of poor judgment on the part of the military was the forceful eviction of residents and shopkeepers along Polk Street. This street was a minor but lively business section then as it is now. For a dozen blocks, the "boys in blue" rapped on the doorways and with bayonets fixed refused to listen to any pleas. This began at 8 A.M. Thursday morning, and the fire didn't reach the street until late that afternoon.

James B. Stetson recorded his feelings shortly after the fire:

"The soldiers lacked good sense and judgment, or perhaps it may have been that some incompetent officers gave senseless orders . . . there was abundant time to save many valuable articles which were by this time lost. Why this was done, I did not understand at the time, nor have I since been able to understand."

The business of caring for hundreds of thousands of hungry, homeless refugees assumed great urgency on the morning of the nineteenth. During the night, Mayor Schmitz transferred his staff from the Fairmont to the North End Police Station. The final move came at 11 A.M. Thursday when the municipal government set up "permanent" temporary headquarters at Franklin Hall on Fillmore Street, more than a mile to the west of the fire lines. It was here that organized civilian relief operations got their start. Eventually, the city fathers

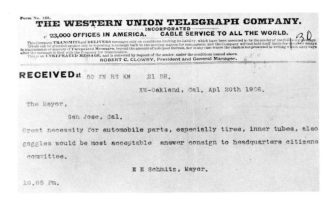

Autos were called "Toys of the Rich" before the fire, but the horseless carriage came of age overnight. (Californiana Collection, San Jose Library)

and their aides were to set up housekeeping in the Whitcomb Hotel on Market Street.

The Army was busy Thursday distributing tents, cots, mattresses, blankets, and hay taken from Army stores. The hay, of course, was to sustain the tens of thousands of horses still quartered in the city.

Some things do not wait for fires to end, and come rain, or snow, or sleet, or hell for that matter, the mails go through. The post office staff, though dead weary from Wednesday's long battle against the fire, began to collect mail Thursday. Everything was makeshift. No normal channels for mail collection or distribution were left. Brief, poignant notes went out of San Francisco on bits and scraps of cardboard, newspaper, old envelopes, even shingles. Anything which carried a message and an address was handled, without postage, as if it were registered mail.

Babies were born during the fire, perhaps at a greater than normal rate. Although the City might be doomed, life went on. One old timer, who tells today of riding shotgun on the last Wells Fargo horse-drawn stage, will also recount the story of the *six* babies he delivered on Market Street during the first day of the fire. Some

North of Union Street on Van Ness weary fire fighters carry on the struggle. The fire burned back across Russian Hill from this point on Friday. (California Historical Society)

babies were indeed born in doorways, and many more beneath the trees in Golden Gate Park and the Presidio before proper homes and hospitals were available.

On Thursday, the first marriage license was issued, one of 220 to be issued in the next ten days at the improvised headquarters of the city clerk.

The fire didn't slow down Thursday, but in most firsthand accounts of the three-and-a-half-day course of the conflagration, most of the emphasis is placed on the first day. And there were good reasons for this: All the well-known buildings in San Francisco went during the first thirty hours. Observers became tired, and the similarity of block after block of devastation in the Mission and on the west side of Nob Hill left little to say. Superlatives had been used up the first day. Photographers had shot much of their film, and the fire lines kept most people far from the action.

Help was on the way. That Thursday the Senate voted $500,000 for aid to San Francisco, and the House upped it to $1 million. Congress eventually appropriated $2½ million for the stricken city. Supplies were already rolling toward San Francisco by Thursday morning from many points. Oakland, that sweet hometown across the bay, never wavered. No questions were asked: her doors were open. To the south, California's second largest incorporated area, Los Angeles, responded with a speed and compassion that all San Franciscans should never forget, no matter what else they may think of that odd town.

While the flames advanced down the west side of Nob Hill and along the six-block front in the Mission, the struggle to establish an orderly routine for existence began. Pestilence, famine, and civil disorder were all feared, but by Thursday the threat of hunger had

The Call=Chronicle=Examiner

SAN FRANCISCO, THURSDAY, APRIL 19, 1906.

EARTHQUAKE AND FIRE: SAN FRANCISCO IN RUINS

| NO HOPE LEFT FOR SAFETY OF ANY BUILDINGS | BLOW BUILDINGS UP TO CHECK FLAMES | WHOLE CITY IS ABLAZE | CHURCH OF SAINT IGNATIUS IS DESTROYED | MAYOR CONFERS WITH MILITARY AND CITIZENS |

This special edition, published without authorization, is perhaps the best loved souvenir of the fire.

OAKLAND ENQUIRER

EXTRA! 6.30 A. M. EXTRA!
An Awful Furnace of Seethinp Flame

The conflagration beyond all control still sweeping onward in its career of destruction wiping out acres of buildings and magnificent homes

SAN FRANCISCO, 5.30 a. m.—At this hour the conflagration continues beyond all control. Heroic efforts to check the onward sweep of the flames are unavailing.

There are two main of the rushing roaring river of flame; one of them working westward drowning block after block of magnificent houses in the western addition and towards the Presidic; while destruction is careering southward down the peninsula into the manufacturing districts in the direction of the Potrero, where there are thousands of workingmen's homes.

The hill section of the city to the west is aflame far beyond Nan Ness avenue and bids fair to sweep on unchecked to the gates of the military reservation and the Richmond district and the sand dunes north of the park.

Southward, only lack of material to feed upon will check the onward sweep of the flames.

Thousands have fled from the flames to the beach beyond the cliff house and Sutro Heights. The roads leading south on the peninsula are black with people with all manner of conveyances fleeing from the doomed city. Even the cemeteries, Cypress Lawn and Holy Cross, are being sought by hundreds as a place of refuge from the flames.

Some of the Touching Scenes	Phelan to Head List With Million	Commendable Action of Building Trades
Witnessed in Connection with the Great San Francisco Fire	Report That He Will Subscribe That Amount For Needy	Will not Countenance Any Increase of Wages in Hour of Misfortune
	Information About Missing Friends	
L. M. HARTLEY DEAD	Many Shot by Guards Across the Bay	Why Red Cross is Not Working as Society

The Enquirer *had the fire racing on toward the Presidio in this edition. Typographical error hints at the pressure and confusion under which newspapers operated. (Bancroft Library)*

passed, minor disorder was rumored but rarely witnessed, and basic sanitation plans had been settled upon.

Food had been commandeered from warehouses and manufacturers, and grocers sold what they had on their shelves as long as they could. In many places, shopkeepers threw open their doors and let the people help themselves to the stock before being driven off by the advancing fire. Food was on its way from outlying towns in the Bay Area, wherever it could be spared, and strong relief committees sprang into being in many cities and towns over the nation. Seventeen carloads of material left Los Angeles on the nineteenth,

Bay view of Telegraph Hill and North Beach fire.

as did the steamship *Roanoke,* loaded with an additional six carloads.

The California Bakery on Fillmore Street, spared by the quake and out of the threatened area, worked on a round-the-clock basis. The San Francisco *Examiner* noted in its issue of April 23, ". . . the big California Baking Company is still doing a noble work. Down in the basements the half-naked bakers are working day and night and every few minutes another great batch of bread is sent into the distribution room."

Strict orders had gone out Wednesday that home plumbing was not to be used, and before the end of the week all of San Francisco was familiar with the details of digging and maintaining latrine trenches.

Many sick and wounded, who on Wednesday had been transferred from the Mechanics Pavilion to improvised outdoor hospitals near the Golden Gate Park panhandle, were carried on Thursday to more suitable quarters at the Presidio.

The exodus from the burned and threatened areas continued on through the second day. The streets leading to the park were thronged with families, and the harsh sound of steamer trunks being dragged along the sidewalks filled the air. The variety of things people carried provoked no end of comment from journalists who watched the scene. "Sewing machines, wads of bedding, pans, dishes, mirrors, crayon portraits, bureaus, beds, pianos, banjos, soup tureens, clogged the sidewalks," wrote novelist Louise Herrick Wall.

Many thousands continued through the Western Addition to the Presidio or the Park or Lafayette or Jefferson squares, leaving their trunks on the western side of Van Ness Avenue as mute evidence of a faith that the big street would not let the fire pass.

Los Angeles, caught up in the frenzied effort to aid San Francisco, suffered a minor shake shortly after noon Thursday, herself. No one was hurt, but as one observer recalls, it ". . . just scared the hell out of everybody."

Rumors remained the main source of "information" until the combined issue of the *Call-Chronicle-Examiner* hit the streets. This issue, put together by homeless San Francisco newspapermen in Oakland without authorization from their publishers, has become the fondest souvenir of the earthquake and fire. The daring and determination of the boys who put it together characterize the whole tone of what the world would soon know as the "indomitable spirit of San Francisco." There's no magic in these words. The "indomitable spirit" was nothing more than fortitude, pride, a smile, and a disinclination to sit down and cry.

In the shingled house which you will find at 1654 Taylor Street today, the tubs were filled with water early Wednesday, April 18, 1906. The Eli T. Sheppard family prepared for a siege, and then made themselves comfortable on the rooftop to watch the burning of San Francisco. Others crowded the hilltop near what today is Ina Coolbrith Park. Thursday morning they were warned to leave by an Army patrol, and with sad hearts joined thousands of others in the trek to the Ferry Building. One person stayed behind. Part of the large house was rented to Mr. E. A. Dakin, a Civil War veteran whose hobby it had been, over the years, to collect American Flags. Mr. Dakin elected to remain in the house. But as the fire pressed closer and the heat grew to the point where the trim began to smoke, Mr. Dakin also gave up hope. Before he went he took the finest flag from his collection, hoisted it up the mast above the house, dipped it three times in a final salute, then departed. A fresh company of the 20th Infantry happened to spot the ceremony from the south side of the Hill. The company, determined not to let such a gesture go unrewarded, stormed up the hill and broke open the door. With water from the tubs, siphon bottles, and wet sand from a construction job across the street, the men held fast against the fire until it had passed. The Sheppards learned of their good fortune a week later when they saw it just as it is in the pictures, unscathed above acres of lonely ashes. (All photos on this page courtesy of Mrs. William E. Hilbert)

Enrico Caruso made sketches of himself watching the fire. (San Francisco Chronicle)

The fire burned through to Jones at Clay and Leavenworth at Sutter by 11:30 Thursday morning. In little more than two hours the fire advanced in a massive front that stretched from Hyde and Clay through the Polk and Sutter. The boom of dynamite explosions on Van Ness punctuated the deep roar of the flames. At 2:30 Van Ness was threatened. The dynamiting continued, and at 3 P.M. backfiring between Washington and Bush began. The method used by the soldiers was simplicity itself. They poured kerosene generously over the floors, lit it, then rushed out and broke windows with rocks and sticks to increase the draft. It took only moments for a house to become a torch. The heat created by the process was, of course, as hot as the enemy fire coming down the hill. Some observers claimed that the backfiring added to the hazard.

The roofs and walls of houses across the wide boulevard smoked in the overpowering heat, and at about six in the evening the thing most feared by the firemen happened: the flames got a foothold on the western side of Van Ness. Somehow falling sparks had set flame to a stable that stood on the grounds of the Claus Spreckels estate near Sacramento, and the fire had been missed until too late. Newspaper accounts tell that tears rolled down the blackened faces of firemen who had toiled without rest for thirty-six hours.

But this fire was held. It burned six blocks between Van Ness and Franklin before the desperate fire fighters brought it under control. Battalion Chief Rudy Schubert, who was to become the last of the 1906 firemen to retire from the department, remembers that he and others in his company pulled smoldering and burning shingles barehanded from roofs to keep the fire from traveling further west.

The battle along Van Ness continued on well into the next day. The fire on the west side of the boulevard was completely under control by 3 A.M., but to the north, where Van Ness retreats toward the Golden Gate, fresh fingers of the fire reached down to threaten the Western Addition. Water was available here, however, and the western side of the street was kept damp while threatening salients, one after the other, were smothered as they drew down toward the broad avenue. Relays of pumping engines carried water from a working hydrant on Buchanan Street to the west, and from the bay to the north.

Earlier in the evening of the nineteenth as all hands watched Van Ness, the fire jumped Washington Street to the north. In all probability, the fire could have been contained south of this street, but no one was there to see it happen. As a result, scores of blocks of houses on Russian Hill and in North Beach were sacrificed. This was the price the city paid to save what lay west of Van Ness Avenue.

Until Friday morning, the fire front along Van Ness ran from St. Mary's Cathedral in the south to Green Street in the north. The fire that had jumped Washington raced through the night eastward across the southern half of Russian Hill, aided by a west wind, which had come up thirty-six hours too late.

Half of Russian Hill and a good part of the North Beach section passed into charred history as the flames swept back toward the east during the night. Friday morning it appeared that Green Street would be the northern boundary of the great fire, but one of the zealous crew who had worked through the preceding day carelessly set off a charge in the Viavi Building on Van Ness near Green, and the flaming embers thrown by the blast set fire to the north side of the street. Reliable observers said later that the fire might have been held at Green had the charge not been set. Perhaps it might have. But the flames had in fact crossed, and in wending their way around the northern side of Russian Hill to the "water" side of North Beach would add another full day to the fire's history.

On Friday the home of Robert Louis Stevenson's widow, at the corner of Hyde and Lombard, was seriously threatened. The house would surely have gone up if it hadn't been for a contingent from the Press and Bohemian clubs headed by Frank Deering. The men arrived in time to douse the house with the dregs from a small reservoir on Russian Hill, using pots, pans, and soaked sacks for weapons.

Henry Lafler sits behind his typewriter in Portsmouth Square near shallow graves across from the Hall of Justice to write his version of the disaster, "My Sixty Sleepless Hours" for McClure's Magazine. Of Portsmouth Square at the moment of the quake he wrote ". . . hysterical women with painted cheeks vomited forth from brothels and dance halls." (California Historical Society)

Saturday's Chronicle *carries good news. "Determination to Rebuild is Everywhere Found" keynotes coming days.*

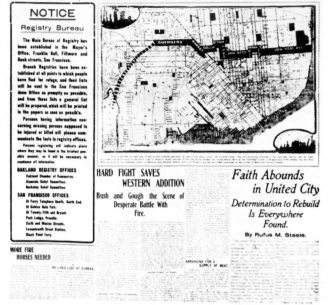

Ina Coolbrith, the poet so dearly loved by her contemporaries, lost her house on Russian Hill in this last gasp of the great fire, as flames curled back up the east side of Russian Hill. The small park which stands today on the site is named for her, but the treasured accumulations of a long and rich life went with the fire.

Yet if you look today on the top of Russian Hill near Ina Coolbrith Park, you will find a cluster of frame houses, between Green and Broadway, Taylor and Leavenworth, which did survive the fire. Partly through circumstance, partly by hard work and luck, these few homes were the only frame structures spared within the 490-block fire area.

The owners of these few blocks had evaded the guards and remained behind to fight off the flames. Using water from cisterns that dated back to a day when the City's system didn't reach that far, the stubborn band fought for hours until dusk Friday. Buckets and brooms and wet towels were their tools. The men nailed wooden cleats to their roofs to make it easier to reach trouble spots. The Sheppard house on Taylor was saved with water stored in bathtubs, with siphon bottles bought the first day of the fire, and wet sand from a construction job across the street. The story of the rescue of this home, told elsewhere in these pages, is one of the best of the fire.

At 3 P.M. on Friday, the fires that had burned eastward on the south and north sides of Russian Hill joined at Columbus Avenue and swept to the sea wall. In the late afternoon the last gasp of this fire burned through the Italian District on Telegraph Hill. Earlier in the day, after the fire crossed Washington, many North Beachers had had to flee the wind-fanned flames. Reports were published that hundreds had perished in the onslaught of the fire, but the story later joined dozens of others on the earthquake-and-fire "fiction shelf."

The men who guarded the Appraiser's Building and had put up the fierce, successful battle against the fire as it approached from the south on Wednesday, had to do it again on Friday when the fire came down off the south slope of Telegraph Hill.

By the evening of the twentieth, only one threat remained. The fires that had burned to the Bay at North Beach threatened to sweep southward along the wharves. The crews of several fireboats and a handful of fire companies fought the fire's advance with all the energy left in them after three days of draining, often frustrating toil. Loss of the docks would have immeasurably hampered the City's recovery. At one time the battle became so intense that the crew of one of the fireboats had to turn the hoses on their own decks to quench fires started by hot embers falling from the sky.

By Saturday morning, the cluster of brick warehouses beneath the eastern bluffs of Telegraph Hill and all the wharves to the south were safe. The struggle to save San Francisco's lifeline—her waterfront—was won.

The fire had run its course.

Genthe's view of City Hall from south slope of Nob Hill. (California Palace of the Legion of Honor)

"THE DAMNDEST FINEST RUINS"

Overlooking Chinatown from California and Stockton. Telegraph Hill, left, Goat Island, right. (California Historical Society)

Countless postcards showing these ruined houses on Howard Street near Eighteenth in the Mission were circulated. The scene was a favorite of photographers after the quake. More serious and more spectacular damage was registered in other sections, but the fire swept most of it away. This section of town was built over loose fill. (Bancroft Library)

RAIN came Saturday evening to lay the ash that covered 490 ravaged blocks. Sunday morning the air was clear except for silvery white traces of steam rising from the damp, hot ruins. Thousands of acres of quiet desolation remained where for three days the worst conflagration in man's history had raged. Never before had so much of man's work been sacrificed to a single fire.

Only scattered marks of a great city remained. The City Hall and its records, the libraries, the courts and jails, the theaters and restaurants had vanished. The heart and guts of one of the world's best loved cities were gone. Thirty schools, eighty churches and convents, the great business sections, and the homes of 250,000 San Franciscans had been taken. Art collections, vast stores of food and goods, 10,000 gardens, the complex transportation and communication systems . . . all these things, big and small, were now part of the City's past.

Businesses had been struck down never to come back. Prominent families had been ruined financially—their names would fade from the public ear and be forgotten. The destruction had been ruthless, unemotional, almost complete. The fire had covered 2831 acres, 490 blocks, and, with the earthquake, claimed more than 450 lives.

Foot of Powell Street, site of today's single downtown cable-car turntable. Flood Building is on the right, the St. Francis Hotel, distant left, and Nob Hill beyond. (California Historical Society)

In the heart of the financial district, the Mills Building stands surrounded by blocks of ruined walls. (California Historical Society)

Looking west over the chaos that was O'Farrell Street. One writer said, "Distance is killed by absence of landmarks and the erasure of high walls; the City appears to have shriveled, it seems no distance between points formerly too far to walk. Squares we thought commodious air spaces have dwindled to insignificant enclosures." (Bancroft Library)

View from Ferry Building looking west on Market, left, and Sacramento, center, taken from a stereoscopic slide. (California Historical Society)

San Francisco's conflagration was at least half again the magnitude of Chicago's banner fire of 1871. Measured in terms of lives, acres, buildings, or dollars, the San Francisco disaster comes out much the worst, with one exception: the winds which had whipped through Chicago carried the flames faster than many had been able to run. Two hundred lives were lost in the race.

Two years before the San Francisco tragedy, America had witnessed another crippling fire when more than eighty-five blocks in the center of Baltimore had burned. But the Baltimore fire didn't even match the London Fire of 1666, while San Francisco's blaze covered *six* times the area of the fabled English calamity. If nothing else, San Francisco had a record which would be hard to beat.

From the hills within the burned area, the streets and squares looked as though a terrible battle had raged across them. Scores of rubble-covered blocks spread out like a gargantuan map, each block distinct and the streets sharply defined.

Still recognizable, Union Square was quick to rebound. It became hub of post-fire activity. Tall frame is Whittell Building. City of Paris is behind Dewey Monument. (Bancroft Library)

View east on Sutter toward shell of St. Dunstan's Hotel on Van Ness. Quake toppled upper walls, dynamite and fire finished the destruction. Joe Foreman, later the San Franciscan everyone knew as Joe Shreve, was doorman. (California Palace of the Legion of Honor)

Until cable cars began to run again months later, there was only one way to get over the hills. Grace Church, a noble ruin, was not rebuilt on this California Street site. (Bancroft Library)

The earthquake tumbled the roof down upon the gallery of the Majestic Theater on Market six hours after its last performance. Fire did not reach the third tier of seats. (Bancroft Library)

Grain wharves at the northern foot of Telegraph Hill burned Friday night and Saturday in the last stages of the fire. Alcatraz Island is on the far right, and Marin County is beyond, through the light fog that covers the Golden Gate.

Arnold Genthe framed desolate ruins on the southern side of Nob Hill in the shattered doorway of what was once a luxurious apartment house. Note heavy steel girder. (California Palace of the Legion of Honor)

In still another Genthe shot taken right after the fire, a solitary Chinese surveys the ruins. Though Chinatown was leveled, optimism and quiet resolve characterized the Chinese reaction. As one old Chinaman said at the Fort Point refugee camp, "Bye and bye, we build all new." (California Historical Society)

View down Dupont Street past Old St. Mary's on the corner of California shows utter ruin of Chinatown. (Bancroft Library)

One of the writers in the *Mining and Scientific Press* wrote this impression of his arrival in the City by ferry:

"On emerging from the Ferry building, one was accustomed to the full-toned voice of a big town, intensified by traffic over the cobbles of Market Street and the confused shouts of hotel runners, the strident cries of newsboys, and the clanging of car bells. All of these are silent; the noises are those of a village; the wagons, express carts, and men on horseback partially screen a ghastly background."

But more of San Francisco was saved than destroyed. The wound was deep, but the patient would live. *Harpers Weekly* pointed out that there remained " . . . the organization of a great city, including the apparatus of government and business, families, traditions, reputations, credits, and established relations with the rest of the world."

Thousands of miles of streets, sewers, and water and gas mains were left with but slight damage. The homes of 150,000 were spared, and the parks and military installations stood untouched. The water front was intact and ready for business. Shipping tonnage in 1906 was to top the preceding year's. The class "A" buildings in the downtown area were sound and strong even though fire

Beyond this pile of steel and brick, twisted and crumbled by temperatures which may have reached 2000 degrees, traffic stirs up dust along Montgomery. Mills Building, left, and Palace Hotel at the end of street. (California Historical Society)

This is the way the wholesale district looked from Telegraph Hill Sunday, the twenty-second, after rain had damp-ened the ashes. Ferry Building, left, Appraiser's Building, right. (California Historical Society)

Globe Flour Mills at the foot of Telegraph Hill might have been saved if soldiers had permitted civilian de-fenders to stay. But orders were orders, and the building burned. (Bear Photo Service)

had raced through almost all of them, leaving behind only the shells of steel and stone, brick and concrete. Al-most all were completely restored before the year was over.

The question: "What if . . . ?" could hardly have been avoided in the days and weeks following the fire. What if the water system hadn't failed? What if dyna-miting had been resorted to earlier? What if dynamiting hadn't been resorted to at all? What if citizens had been allowed to defend their own homes? What if the west wind had come up earlier? What if Chief Sullivan had been able to take charge? The answers to these and all the other questions were meaningless to the stricken city, but it is the nature of humankind to dwell, sometimes, on what-might-have-been. The real value of such in-quiry would be in its crystallization of the wisdom and insight born of the whole, harsh experience.

There is no question that the dynamiters did little if any good. With the exception of the expert work done by the Mare Island team along Van Ness on Friday, none of the blasting seemed to have done anything but set buildings on fire and break windows. Black powder and dynamite in the hands of amateurs proved worse than none at all.

Arnold Genthe's landscape of Telegraph Hill from Nob Hill. (California Palace of the Legion of Honor)

Somber portrait of the Ferry Building taken before the rush of debris clearing and reconstruction began. Although it appears deserted, the ferries never halted service, and traffic was heavier than ever at fire's end. (Bancroft Library)

RIGHT: Union Street cuts across Polk to Van Ness and on into the unscathed Western Addition. Golden Gate, distant right. The fire's boundaries traced a line close to the limits of the City's first incorporated area. Old San Francisco was bounded by Larkin on the west and Eighteenth on the south. (California Historical Society)

Across the burned section of the Mission, two- and three-story frame houses crowd the Howard Street boundary. You can see the tilted houses shown in close-up on page 82. Nineteenth Street lies on the right. Some hurried construction had begun, left. (California Palace of the Legion of Honor)

Chronicle and Call buildings, framework of the Whittell Building, Grace Church, and the Fairmont Hotel are most easily recognized landmarks in this sweeping scene taken Sunday from Telegraph Hill. Center picture shows the Montgomery Block—Idwal Jones' Ark of Empire—on the right. Row of buildings to the left was also spared. (California Historical Society)

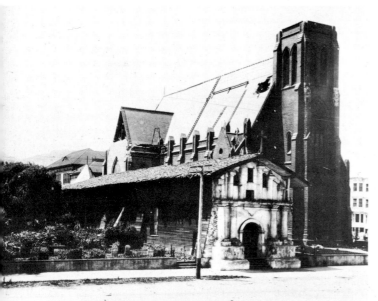

What might have happened if experts had taken charge during the first morning still remains a question. S. B. Christy, Dean of the College of Mines at the University of California said, "A hundred California miners, used to handling dynamite, could have saved three fourths of the burned district by intelligent and prompt blasting." He added that Chinatown should have been leveled during the afternoon Wednesday.

The lack of water is commonly supposed to have been the ultimate reason San Francisco burned down. Hundreds of breaks in the mains and thousands of broken house connections drained off in an incredibly short time the millions of gallons stored within the City. The conduits from Crystal Springs and Pilarcitos reservoirs in San Mateo County to the south were, with a single exception, all broken. Aside from the water that remained in the mains the first morning, the reservoirs of San Francisco supplied no water for fire fighting during the first thirty-six hours. The Lake Merced system had been hastily repaired and this water supplied help in the defense at Van Ness. Many buildings, many blocks, perhaps whole sections might have been saved if unlimited water had been available. But the experts denied this. "The breaking of the mains handicapped

Mission Dolores is dwarfed by the newer church, but it survived while the bigger structure had to be torn down. (Bancroft Library)

Tangled steel and plaster drape the gutted frame of the Emporium Building. (California Historical Society)

Nothing was left of the fire house where Chief Sullivan was mortally injured. His headquarters stood next to the California Theater and Hotel, left, on Bush Street. The engine house was rebuilt on the same spot, and a plaque commemorating Sullivan's passing has been placed on the façade. Mills Building in the distance. (Bancroft Library)

"A very few people were to be seen among the ruins, which added much to the general gloom of the situation. I found it difficult then," said James B. Stetson, "and ever since, very difficult to locate myself when wandering in the ruined district, as all the old landmarks are gone." Picture on the left of the Hearst Building at Market and Third taken by Arnold Genthe. (California Palace of the Legion of Honor)

"Portals of the Past" was the name given the remains of the Towne Mansion on Nob Hill. Arnold Genthe framed the City Hall between the simple Ionic columns of the entrance. James D. Phelan, a leader in the rebuilding of the City, had the columns taken down and reassembled on the shore of Lloyd Lake in Golden Gate Park. (California Palace of the Legion of Honor)

them, of course," said the Boston *Evening Transcript,* "but it is doubtful if they could have coped with the conflagration even though they had plenty of water."

When one considers that only 585 firemen with few more than fifty pieces of equipment—steam engines, hooks and ladders, and chemical units—faced the mile-wide fire front without water, without the leadership of their chief, and without adequate communications, it is not difficult to see why the City couldn't be saved. A committee investigating for the insurance companies had this to say:

"It would at least be doubtful if even in New York a dozen simultaneous fires could be successfully suppressed if scattered through a territory a mile long and a quarter of a mile wide, in spite of the fact that New York could concentrate more than three times the amount of apparatus at the points of danger."

The dire prediction of the Board of Fire Underwriters a year before had nailed the facts to the wall for all to see:

"San Francisco has violated all underwriting traditions and precedents by not burning up; that it has not done so is largely due to the vigilance of the fire department, which cannot be relied upon indefinitely to stave off the inevitable."

City Hall was, as one observer saw, ". . . now a ruin, noble with a beauty that it had lacked when entire." Built over a period of 20 years, the big structure varied in quality of construction from one political regime to the next. (Bancroft Library)

A sailor stands guard with bayonet fixed on California Street between Mason and Taylor overlooking the downtown section. The Call Building can be seen on the far right, and the top of Grace Church tower is barely visible above sidewalk, far left. An Arnold Genthe photo. (California Palace of the Legion of Honor)

View down Stockton to Market on Sunday, April 22. Every phase of life was reduced to a primitive level. If proportional damage had been wreaked on New York City, all the island of Manhattan from the Battery to 125th Street, a few stray buildings excepted, would have been leveled. Actually, the destroyed area was equal to what lies within New York's Fifth and Ninth avenues between Twenty-third and 103rd streets. (Bancroft Library)

West on Sutter from Market. Earthquake and dynamite did their damage, but neither reduced the steel, stone, and brick of the City's business district to the utter shambles you have seen on these pages—it was the fire. "Square blocks of granite were reduced to rounded boulderlike forms . . . Marble pillars were quickly converted to caustic lime," reported the Mining and Scientific Press. "Even sandstone . . . cracked and crumbled before the fiery blast. Steel and iron were warped and bent, and in some instances they were even melted. Nothing resisted the intense heat but good brick." (Bancroft Library)

Northwest from Kearny through Portsmouth Square. (California Palace of the Legion of Honor)

LIFE

GOES

ON

Sight-seeing was the outdoor sport when fire ended. A cameraman pauses on the California Street cable-car tracks and looks toward the Merchant's Exchange. Old St. Mary's is on the near left. (Bancroft Library)

High society airs its bedding in Golden Gate Park. Note the blanketed horses and fancy brougham. (Edward Zelinsky)

Workingman's family spreads bedding in Lobos Square. (Bear Photo Service)

THE rest of the nation had swung into action before the ashes had a chance to settle. Food, medicines, cots, and blankets were the vanguard of hundreds of tons of relief supplies that would pour into the City. In the matter of a handful of days $8 million had been raised to help San Francisco in the staggering task of starting anew. And in the months to follow, another million would be added to that. Never before had the American public responded as it did in 1906.

Harper's Weekly said this in answer to those who might have wondered why the response had been so generous:

"It is because all warm-hearted Americans who have known her, or have read her history, have long looked upon San Francisco as Columbia's most lovable and fairest child . . . the civilization evolved by the Argonauts . . . was so blithe, so jocund, so exhilarating; so naive in its exultation, so artless in the frank expression of its just and contagious complacency, that no warm-blooded visitor could find room in his soul for criticism, much less detraction, but felt a responsive shiver of admiration and affection . . . So when it came to pass that these men and women who seemed born for rejoicing were staggered all at once by an appalling cataclysm, is it any wonder that the nation's heart was wrung?"

96

Sailors help relief officials hand out emergency supplies while the fire still rages. Orderly breadlines replaced scenes like this even before the fire had ended. Food was commandeered from wholesale and retail stocks, but before many days, ample supplies came into the City by rail to forestall any possibility of famine. (Edward Zelinsky)

Could *Harper's Weekly* have been far wrong about a city where the people thronged to the only remaining theater—the Chutes out near Golden Gate Park at Tenth Avenue and Fulton Street—only *eight* days after the fire to see and hear and laugh at Orpheum performers in a show complete with trick cyclists, a blackface skit, and a one-act *Carmen* in memory of the last performance at the Opera House. A new march by E. M. Rosner called "Greater San Francisco" was dedicated to Mayor Schmitz and played for the first time at the same performance.

Could *Harper's Weekly* have been far wrong when the world read Lillian Ferguson's story in the *Examiner,* written the day after the fire ended?

"It was raining yesterday when I passed an Italian woman sitting on a pile of bricks that was once the home of a friend of mine. In her arms was a wailing infant.

'No milk here since the earthquake scare me so hard,' she explained in difficult English, pointing to her breast.

A fat, motherly young Irishwoman with a bouncing boy on her arm stopped on her weary journey to the ferry.

'I've got enough for two,' she laughed. 'Give me the kid. There darlint, take your dinner.' And Italy drained the milk of human kindness from Erin's fount."

Aid from the coast cities arrived first—cars from Los Angeles, Seattle, Stockton, and Sacramento reached the City before the fire died out. From Vancouver to San Diego, food was on its way. Within the week, trains

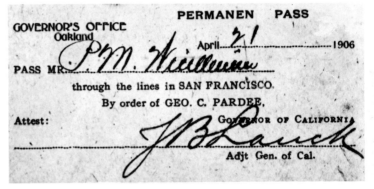

Passes were freely issued to all who had legitimate business within the fire lines. (Max H. Willemin)

Italians pause to eat on the trek to refuge. (Bancroft Library)

97

Water for drinking was scarce in the first days after the fire. Much of it was brought across the Bay on barges, and in some cases, it was pumped into barrels and tank wagons by hand. Here, the man in charge tips the barrel to get the last drop. Ferry Building, far right. (Edward Zelinsky)

The misdeeds of a few soldiers reflected badly on the Army, and friction and mistrust grew. Headlines like this did not help smooth the situation. Story at bottom of the page describes an accidental shooting.

arrived from all over. Some of the boxcars carried signs:

"FOR THE CALIFORNIA SUFFERERS

FROM DENVER, COLORADO—MORE TO FOLLOW"

"FROM BURLINGTON, IOWA"

"FROM BUFFALO, NEW YORK"

"FRESH MEAT FROM COALINGA"

A. R. Springer, chairman of Sacramento relief, arrived with a steamer and bargeload of provisions and the message that he was ready to carry refugees back to the capital city and then return with more supplies.

A man struggles over the cobblestones with part of a shoe-shine stand loaded on a child's wagon to help, in his own small way, get the City back on its feet. (California Historical Society)

At the beginning, the Army handed out supplies with no attempt to account for the material. This line-up of ladies in Golden Gate Park is an interesting study of types. Ample lady on the right does not appear to be in a trifling mood.
(Edward Zelinsky)

He ended his announcement to the San Francisco authorities with this magnanimity:

"San Francisco can count on Sacramento for the last bit of bread and meat in the house, can draw on us for every dollar we have, and then you can have our blood if you need it."

In Ogden, Utah, no bread was to be had for days—all went to San Francisco. Children there, as in many towns, were excused from school to collect food.

Boys of the Chemewa, Oregon, Indian School bought flour with their savings and baked 830 loaves of bread for San Francisco. The bread was sent by Wells Fargo Express and reached the City on Saturday the twenty-first.

The New York City Merchants Association ordered fourteen carloads of foodstuffs by long-distance telephone to be sent from Omaha. They sent $60,000 worth of drugs in the first week, and much clothing later. In all, New York City raised more than $185,000 for San Francisco. For days, Salvation Army lassies stood on corners of the big town with placards reading:
"FOR THE SAN FRANCISCO SUFFERERS."

In one month 1800 carloads of supplies came into the City on the Southern Pacific tracks.

To no one's surprise, the entertainment world turned out to help the stricken City:

The Barnum and Bailey Circus contributed a day's receipts—$20,000.

Mission Park was crowded with South of Market refugees after the fire marshall ordered Mission residents who had slept there during the fire to the Castro Street Hills. Church on the far right stands next to Mission Dolores on Dolores Street. Mission High School faces on Eighteenth Street.
(Bear Photo Service)

Half truths and ambiguities enliven the headlines in this issue of April 24. There was no rioting in San Francisco, although the story accurately tells of conflict between the police and the soldiers on duty. Ghoul story at bottom of page relates the tale of a man who asked permission to take one last look at the body of his mother lying on a pile of corpses. Soldiers shot the man, according to the tale, when they found him chewing the earrings off the dead woman's ears. Under the word "RIOTS" is a widely circulated story of the three men trapped by fire on a downtown roof who were shot as an act of mercy by the soldiers. Story was never corroborated. By this date, stories other than those of the San Francisco tragedy began to make the front pages.

Sarah Bernhardt held one benefit performance on April 26 in Chicago and gave another in the Greek Theater on the University of California campus in May.

George M. Cohan sold papers on Wall Street— some of them going for as high as $1000.

Down in Los Angeles, men with megaphones climbed into boxes to exhort passers-by for pennies and gold pieces. Jim Jeffries, the retired heavyweight champ sold oranges from a wagon in town to raise $600. Stage favorites and other well-known personalities performed in assorted stunts and sold newspapers on the streets to raise cash. As the Los Angeles relief report noted:

"One who passed along the principal business streets of Los Angeles during the first three days following the San Francisco earthquake, not knowing the circumstances, might have concluded that the population had gone mad." Los Angeles authorities met on the first day of the fire after it became obvious that large-scale relief would be required. They wired Mayor Schmitz a promise of $100,000, and immediately diverted to San Francisco the money raised a week before the relief of Vesuvius victims. On the twentieth, at the suggestion of a man named Joseph Desmond, "cooking camps" were ordered for the City. The outfits, which cost $500 each, were designed to serve simple, hot meals. ". . . one of the most effective relief measures in all the work done in behalf of the sufferers," commented one reporter.

By Saturday April 21, seventy-five carloads had been shipped, or were ready for shipment, to San Francisco.

The City of Angels was unstinting through the weeks following the disaster. She left only one blot on the ledger:

During the summer, postcards and pamphlets were circulated by unknown parties showing San Francisco

Everyone seems to be having a good time in this shot, except, perhaps, the flour-covered Mack Sennett cop in the center. Although there were a few complaints about the police getting the best of things, the City police force came in for very little criticism for their conduct during and after the fire. (Morton-Waters Company)

These men are digging through the debris for canned goods, and two of them, extreme right and left, are opening their find. The same picture was carried in the Illustrated London News *of May 26, 1906, with the caption: "Searching the Debris for Killed and Wounded."* (Bancroft Library)

in ruins with the legend, "Los Angeles was not affected in the least by the San Francisco earthquake." Some said that Los Angeles real estate men were behind the scheme. Although the L. A. Chamber of Commerce self-righteously condemned the material as "unjust," the very same Chamber had earlier published this modest story:

"On April 20 a telegram was received from Philadelphia asking if Los Angeles needed help. A proper answer was sent, reading as follows: 'No sympathy needed here. Not affected in any manner here by the earthquake. Citizens Relief Committee of Los Angeles raising a quarter of a million dollars for San Francisco and vicinity.'"

Some ate in style, although the fare was the same for all. Looking east from Van Ness to Turk. (Bear Photo Service)

Soldiers indulge in a bit of horseplay as they watch the breadline on Sixth Street between Mission and Market. (Bancroft Library)

People in many other parts of the world collected relief funds, despite Teddy Roosevelt's announcement that the U. S. Government would not transmit money to San Francisco from foreign nations. The President's strange pronouncement caused no little head-scratching and grumbling in the American press.

The Japanese Red Cross and Government contributed more than half the total from all sources outside the U.S. Here's the foreign box score:

Japan	$244,960.10
Canada	145,412.65
China	40,000.00
France	21,235.08
Mexico	14,480.31
England	6,570.88
Cuba	734.30
Australia	385.96
Russia	199.02
Scotland	50.40
Austria	50.00
Belgium	50.00
Germany	50.00
Ceylon	32.33
	$474,211.03

Gathering the $9 million for relief was relatively easy. But spending that money to best advantage was

This octagonal house, one of several in San Francisco, was built at the corner of Union and Gough in 1864. In the picture, taken by Arnold Genthe, the Cavagnaro family sorts through a wagonload of old clothes. (California Palace of the Legion of Honor)

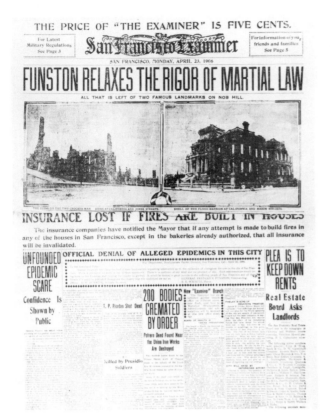

The police have given permission to sort through the debris of an old warehouse for cups, household goods. (Bear Photo Service)

The Examiner, *like the other San Francisco dailies, published Monday making only the barest reference to its own troubles. One story tells of a soldier shooting a young man who, when stopped on his way home, refused to throw away a bottle of whisky. Funston's order meant that no property could be commandeered nor could any citizen be pressed into labor without an order from headquarters.*

not quite so simple. Teddy Roosevelt said that the ". . . outpouring of the Nation's aid should be entrusted to the Red Cross," and Secretary of War William Howard Taft, president of that organization, took charge.

His first act was to appoint Dr. Edward T. Devine, an experienced relief administrator from New York, as his personal representative. Devine's appointment evoked disappointment and some grousing among San Francisco leaders, since on the surface it appeared to show a lack of confidence in the ability of San Francisco to run its own affairs. The matter was quickly

Butchers cut up fresh meat for distribution at the corner of Laguna and Jackson. The mansion on the left was the home of W. P. Fuller's partner in the paint business, W. F. Whittier. It later served as Nazi German consulate under the notorious Fritz Wiedemann, and is now headquarters for the California Historical Society. (Bancroft Library)

San Jose paper tells of disease threat. Rumors on the subject reached the public through many published reports, but there was no basis for them. Dr. Ward, Chairman of the Health Committee made this announcement: "Say to the people of California, of the U.S. and of the world that there is no epidemic in San Francisco. . . . The sanitation of the city is absolutely under control. I wish to impress this on the people of San Francisco and of the outside world; for I have information that leads me to believe that alarmist reports emanating from certain sources in San Francisco may result in an embargo being placed on the movement of refugees from the city. The calamity we have endured is certainly sufficient without adding to this additional and unwarranted distress." General Funston sent the telegram below in answer to a frightened query from San Jose, also badly damaged by the quake. (Californiana Collection, San Jose Library)

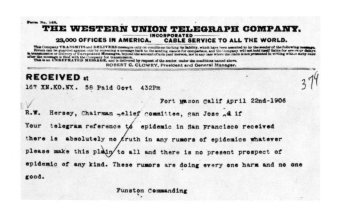

Emigration from the ruined city continued for weeks after the fire. Here a well-loaded wagon approaches Third and Market on its way to the Ferry. Call Building, right. (Edward Zelinsky)

forgotten once Devine arrived. San Francisco soon learned that he had the tact, experience, and energy required for the job.

Devine reported to General Greely, who had rushed back from the East to take over command of the Army from Funston on April 23. The two agreed on division of authority: the Red Cross was to handle all direct relief while the Army was to guard the property and health of the City and provide for transport of supplies. Up until this time, the emergency had required "crash" measures to feed the hungry and to provide the rudiments of comfort to the homeless. During the fire, the Army and the mayor's committee commandeered food and supplies without stopping to answer questions.

On Saturday, the City's wholesale grocers met at Franklin Hall on Fillmore to settle on the best plan for concerted action. By the twenty-fifth, many were back in business. Michael Casey, head of the Teamsters, agreed with the mayor's transportation committee on a plan to systematize draying, and before the end of the week of the twenty-third, food distribution had settled to a routine.

At one time, 150 relief stations were in operation, doling out bread, canned meat, coffee, potatoes, and

The auto was the "unquestioned hero of the San Francisco fire," said Century magazine, and there was little doubt about it. On the morning of the eighteenth it was used as an ambulance and a hearse, and later every available car was commandeered to transport doctors, messengers, officials of the Mayor's committee, medicine, food, and other supplies. Many of the cars carried signs—DYNAMITE, POLICE, AMBULANCE—and until the Signal Corps rigged up an emergency semaphore and telephone system, the auto was the only practical means of communication. In the picture at the top of the page, a volunteer chauffeur smiles into the camera as he parks in front of a relief station in Pacific Heights. Among other things, autos were used to gather hose for defense of the water front. One writer said, "There will probably never in the history of automobiles be a time when they accomplish so much," and the Overland Monthly in an article titled "Triumph of the Automobile" stated: "While beloved San Francisco was being devastated last April the automobile was making the greatest record in history. Without its aid, the damage done the city would have been far greater, and the sufferings of the inhabitants would have been immeasurably increased."
(California Historical Society; Bancroft Library)

Troops guarding the lines on Montgomery Street strike a military pose and gaze off toward Market. (California Historical Society)

Outdoor kitchens were a necessity in San Francisco for weeks and months. Note indifferent horse on sidewalk. (California Historical Society)

Uncle Sam points to the example of Chicago and Baltimore in this typical post-fire editorial cartoon.

other staples on a day-to-day basis. The food that poured into the City even before the fire ended forestalled the possibility of famine, although such rumors made headlines in some out-of-state newspapers.

No one was given preference, and there was very little complaining. The well-to-do who still had money found nothing to buy with it. All food was obtained by standing in line for it, and for several weeks, the wealthy rubbed elbows with workingmen. Bread was the first staple that could be purchased. Other staples became available on May 3—a date as good as any other to mark the resumption of normal intercourse in the City.

The amount spent by relief authorities for food in the first months is a good indication of the speed with which normal channels were re-established. In the first

An intimate family scene caught by Arnold Genthe on Franklin Street near Sutter, looking toward Nob Hill. (California Palace of the Legion of Honor)

More potatoes were given to the City than could be eaten. Sale of surplus donations netted about $250,000. (California Historical Society)

Relief workers pose in a Pacific Heights backyard relief station. Barrel contains corned beef from Baltimore. (California Historical Society)

three weeks following the earthquake, $730,000 was spent for relief of the hungry, while no more than $75,000 was spent in any four-week period later. Food and other necessities had to be paid for by somebody, and individuals were expected to begin paying for what they received—if they had the price. This was to be the simple, common-sense guide used through the whole rehabilitation period.

On July 20, civic leaders incorporated the San Francisco Relief and Red Cross Funds Committee, with James D. Phelan as president. Subcommittees formed under the direction of the committee's twenty-one directors were staffed with volunteer help. Although the Army had already doled out much of the Congressional appropriation in the form of food, tents, blankets, hay for horses, medical supplies and other necessities,

This photo of a Red Cross committee in action came from an album prefaced with a note by Mrs. Albert Woodburn Scott: "A souvenir of a time we shall never forget." (California Historical Society)

Easygoing soldier's antics bring smiles along this breadline in Golden Gate Park. (Bancroft Library)

People of all stations mixed in the relief lines, without discrimination. Potatoes are piled in the foreground. (California Historical Society)

the painstaking task of placing dollars where they would do the most good began. If all the relief money left unspent after the critical emergency period, say $7 million, were divided evenly among San Francisco's 400,000, it would have amounted to something less than $18 a person—not much with which to start a new life, even at 1906 prices.

The patient, hard-working relief people were to get a lot of mileage out of the $7 million in the next two years.

As the relief program was being formed, the city government set about restoring its normal functions. Most of the fire equipment had been rescued, but it took weeks to get the water system back into working order. Vigilance was the major weapon against fire in

Looking in these faces, one cannot doubt that "the resiliency of the human spirit," as Out West magazine put it, has never been better demonstrated in time of peace. (Bancroft Library)

that period. No one was allowed to cook indoors, and all food, aside from that prepared at the large relief kitchens, was cooked over improvised street ranges. Some of the outdoor "barbeques" consisted of nothing more than a few bricks—there was an abundance to be had for the picking—and a scrap of sheet metal or perhaps a grill from the kitchen range. The insurance companies warned Mayor Schmitz that all insurance still in effect in that part of the City which had survived would be cancelled if indoor cooking were permitted. It took many months to inspect all the standing chimneys, and not until the last chimney had been pronounced safe did outdoor kitchens disappear from the streets. This phase of the post-fire period has remained one of the fond recollections of all survivors.

The insurance companies had a lot more than the threat of another fire to worry about. No one knew in 1906 just how much the loss by fire amounted to in dollars and cents. And no one knows today. The best-qualified guessers put the figure between $350 and and $500 million—not an inconsiderable sum when you

Wednesday, the twenty-fifth, the Call told the story of the disarming of the special police who had been sworn to duty during the fire. Hysterical exaggerations have given away to a more sober consideration of the task at hand.

Even before the rubble had been cleared from Market Street, two-way traffic replaced the one-way line of fleeing refugees that jammed the great thoroughfare in the later days of the fire. Much business was temporarily transferred to Oakland, and commute traffic stepped up briskly. In this view to the east, the familiar Palace Hotel and Call Building stand on the left, with the Crocker Building beyond the intersection to the right. Picture was taken the week of the twenty-third. (Bancroft Library)

The Hibernian Bank escaped with relatively light damage from earthquake and fire, and was the scene of much activity after the fire. Once depositors had been allowed to withdraw what they needed, the police took over the building as temporary headquarters. Here, officers and employees of the bank who stood guard over the bank during the height of the fire gather for a formal portrait. (Edward Zelinsky)

Stereoscope slide of the Hamilton Square Post Office Station. It is a remarkable fact that not a piece of mail was lost in the disaster. Forty years later, veteran Post Office employee, Martin J. O'Donnell, told Robert O'Brien that the closest call came when a streetcar carrying mail at the time of the quake caught fire and burned. The sacks were dragged off in time, though, to keep the record clean. (California Historical Society)

remember that it takes perhaps six of today's dollars to build what one dollar would then. The highest estimate of loss was $1 billion . . . almost twice the federal expenditures that year.

Guessing aside, the important fact to burned-out property owners then was that a hundred-odd insurance companies had written between $225 and $250 million worth of insurance on the destroyed buildings. This money was to form the heart of the bankroll which would rebuild the City.

Never before had the fire-insurance industry faced such a challenge, nor has it since. One of the first steps

Homeless men, wearing the only clothes they own, rummage through donated suits and coats at Jefferson Square. (Bear Photo Service)

Proprietors of the Western Addition Oyster and Chop House were, like everyone else, forced to cook in the street. (California Historical Society)

the companies took was to set up a central adjustment bureau. The chaos was almost humorous: some people had lost the policies or the documents needed to establish proof of loss, and worse than that, some of the insurance companies had lost all their records. Some claimants couldn't even remember the name of the company that had written the policy they had lost in the fire. In short, confusion and uncertainty ruled.

Slowly, as the days and weeks passed, it dawned on claimants that not all the insurance companies were going to settle without stalling and using every means to whittle down the size of the adjustment. For some, all that remained were the clothes on their backs, a few meager handouts from the relief agencies, and an insurance policy. It can be honestly said that the only unanimous carping San Francisco was guilty of in all the days during or following the calamity was the fully justified campaign of complaint against the insurance companies.

Groups were formed to protect otherwise helpless policy holders from unfair treatment, and to carry on a vocal campaign of denunciation. The issue attracted national attention.

Congress listened sympathetically to a speech delivered on June 28, 1906, by the Honorable Julius Kahn of San Francisco, "The San Francisco Disaster—Honest and Dishonest Insurance." His title was appropriate, for there were honest companies among the others. To quote the report of the National Association of Credit Men on the settlements made by the various companies: ". . . the people of San Francisco received their greatest aid in obtaining honest and liberal adjustments, from honorable and fearless insurance companies which refused to be parties to agreements for arbitrary deductions, and which paid their losses amounting to millions of dollars in a spirit of liberality and honesty."

Only six companies made adjustments quickly and then paid off in full without delay and without asking cash discount. They were:

1. Aetna Insurance Company, Hartford, Connecticut
2. California Insurance Company, San Francisco, California
3. Continental Insurance Company, New York, New York
4. Liverpool, London and Globe Insurance Company, Liverpool, England
5. Queen Insurance Company of America, New York, New York
6. Royal Insurance Company, Liverpool, England

Umbrellas and parasols were up this Sunday to protect parishoners of St. Dominic's at Bush and Pierce from the heat of the sun. Many churches had to hold out-of-door services for months while damage surveys and repairs could be made. The houses of worship of all faiths— Catholic, Protestant, and Jewish were opened to public activity wherever the buildings were safe. Calvary Presbyterian Church, St. Mary's Cathedral, and Temple Sherith-Israel, all to the west of Van Ness, were the largest to survive. Bishop Montgomery conducted Mass at the cathedral on the Sunday following the fire. (California Historical Society)

Phoenix rises above flames on cover of a forgotten song. (Bancroft Library)

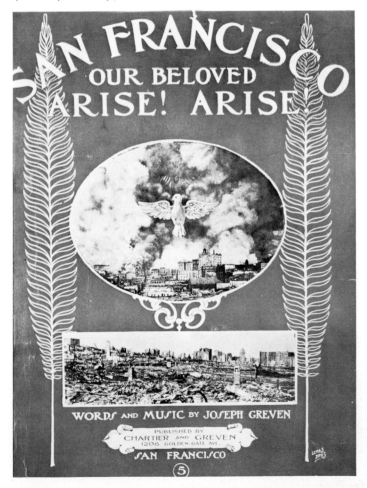

This temporary kitchen was operated at the corner of Laguna and Jackson streets in first weeks after the fire. Note the Whittier mansion in the background, upper left. The young lady at the end of the counter discovered the photographer while he was shooting, and couldn't keep her eyes away. Men eat as if they hadn't seen food in days. (Bancroft Library)

Downtown, in Union Square, the ladies of a social group hold a benefit. As is often true in such affairs, the participants are well meaning and manage to have a fine time for themselves. Last frame shows the St. Francis Hotel. (Bancroft Library)

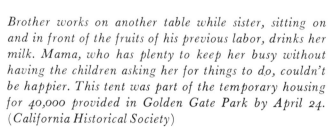

Brother works on another table while sister, sitting on and in front of the fruits of his previous labor, drinks her milk. Mama, who has plenty to keep her busy without having the children asking her for things to do, couldn't be happier. This tent was part of the temporary housing for 40,000 provided in Golden Gate Park by April 24. (California Historical Society)

In addition, the Hartford Fire Insurance Company promptly paid off a whopping $10 million with a 2% discount for cash. Many other companies came close to matching this fine record. It is sad to note, however, that more did not. Here is a box score compiled from the extensive report of the credit men:

Ranking	American	English	German	Other
TOPS	19	12	0	0
GOOD—a 2% to 5% cash deduction after adjustment	12	1	0	1 (New Zealand)
POOR — anywhere from a 5% to 10% deduction to a complete default.	43	6	6	4 (1 Austrian, 1 Swedish, 2 Canadian)

It is not strange that two San Francisco companies left the most memorable records. One, the California Fire Insurance Company, had assets of $450,000 at the time, but its gross liability as a result of the fire was

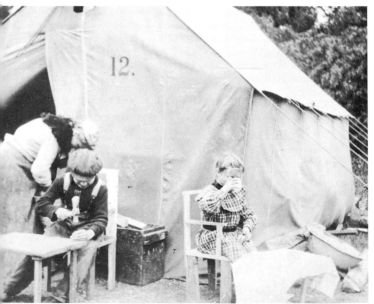

$2,550,000. The company promptly assessed its stockholders the difference, and it paid off every cent owed. This forthright action prompted the Credit Men to say, "If other companies had emulated the California Insurance Company, an impressive record would have been made in the annals of fire insurance."

Fireman's Fund Insurance Company perhaps deserves as much praise as those which were given an excellent rating. This company faced the job of settling more than $11½ million in claims, and there was little more than $7 million in total assets with which to pay. Rather than divide up what was left among the policy holders and then fold their tent for good, the directors buried the proud old San Francisco company and formed a new corporation—free of the burden of debt. Claimants of the defunct Fireman's Fund Insurance Company were offered 56½% cash and 50% stock in the new corporation against their claims. The Policy Holders League, whose only reason for being was to battle the insurance companies, had this to say:

"The Committee feels that the Officers in rehabili-

tating the Fireman's Fund Insurance Company, and restoring it to such a strong financial position have, through admirable pluck and fair dealing, won a splendid victory—honorable to both the Company and to the Community—over tremendously adverse circumstances, and that the Company has proven itself entitled to the confidence, good-will and patronage of the insuring public."

Unfortunately, the record of other companies leaves this an unhappy chapter. Six German companies treated their San Francisco obligations with contempt. Three of them, along with a lone Austrian Company, denied all responsibility and withdrew from business in this country. They deserved the "keenest censure" in the words of the Credit Men's Report. Another of the companies, the Hamburg-Bremen Fire Insurance Company settled most of its $4½ million in losses with arbitrary discounts of 20% and 25%. But the welching wasn't enough. The Credit Men added this about the Hamburg-Bremen Company:

"It was severely criticized for insulting and discour-

The Mills Building and the Fairmont Hotel rear up above a photographer who prefers to focus on a less spectacular part of the ruin. Donahue Fountain is on the far left. The photo was taken from Bush and Market streets. (California Historical Society). RIGHT: *Van Ness Avenue was blocked off at Eddy while debris was cleared and repairs were made to the street. (California Historical Society)*

teous treatment, and also for displaying in its New York office a misleading notice, to the effect that it was pleased to inform its friends and patrons that funds had been sent over from Hamburg for the purpose of promptly paying its San Francisco losses."

If it is any consolation to those who might fret about the record of the German companies, only three American firms ignored earthquake clauses in the policies which might have excused them from liability, and two of the three were German-American companies.

Among the American Companies that emerged with

Sidewalk kitchens were many things: "A few bricks with an oven grate . . . a handsome nickled range within a spacious shed . . . a tiny round stove called 'The Palace Grill,'" said Outlook *magazine recounting this relatively pleasant phase of post-fire life. It has been claimed, facetiously, that today's outdoor cooking mania has its roots in the 1906 fire aftermath. Tens of thousands of "barbeques" were set up in the streets, but no one left the comfort of his home, in those sensible days, merely to comply with a fad. (California Palace of the Legion of Honor)*

Lotta's Fountain, given to the City by Lotta Crabtree in 1875, survives to this day, a homely monument at one of the busiest corners—Kearny, Geary, and Market. (Bancroft Library)

Another compassionate tableau by Arnold Genthe. This one, taken in the Park a few weeks after the fire, shows the elementary level to which life was reduced. The father hauls water, older sister stirs the pot, and mother sews on a rescued machine to build the family wardrobe and, perhaps, to earn a little money. (California Palace of the Legion of Honor)

Judge's humor might have missed the mark, but there is no mistaking the artist's good intention. (Bancroft Library)

"bad" reputations, it should be noted that many assessed their stock holders to the limit in attempts to meet their obligations.

Twelve companies, all American, either failed or retired from business by reason of the fire.

Fire threats and reneging insurance companies were just a few of the things San Franciscans had to worry about in those hectic days following the fire. Although the police set up shop at Lowell High School and began the job of restoring local control, the military forces were needed for more than a month.

The troops created a certain amount of ill will in the first days by forcing men at the point of a bayonet to work at clearing the streets. When John Drew, the distinguished actor, heard that his nephew John Barrymore had been ordered to stack bricks, he commented:

THE EARTH—"I HOPE I SHALL NEVER HAVE ONE OF THOSE SPLITTING HEADACHES AGAIN."

"Calamity is man's true touchstone," wrote Beaumont and Fletcher more than 300 years ago. The words, which were recalled by Eloise Roorbach and painted into a cover for Overland Monthly *epitomized not only the courage shown by San Franciscans in the dark hours, but their gallant good humor in the face of hardship. The "House of Mirth," in this widely circulated photo taken at Jefferson Square, was named for a popular novel by Edith Wharton. (Morton-Waters Company)*

Although this April 27 headline—like those a week before—is largely hot air, falling walls and aftershocks did create a hazard. One man was reported injured when he jumped through the window of his home in fright when a small tremor hit on the evening of April 23, and the Independent *told of a woman being killed by a falling chimney toppled by a shock on April 25.*

"It took a convulsion of a nation to get Jack out of bed and the United States Army to get him to work."

Despite lighter moments, the Army's high-handedness became so flagrant at times that Mayor Schmitz was impelled to officially remind the Army that the City was not under martial control.

The militia and the "specials" came in for particularly strong criticism as time wore on. While the fire burned, rumors spread that troops were shooting all who were found in even the smallest transgression. After the facts had a chance to sift through, it became apparent that the "twenty to one hundred" killed by the soldiers was an exaggeration. A conservative report puts the total dead by violence at nine:

"Two killed by the Nat'l Guard, one by a member of a so called Citizens vigilance committee, one by a police officer, one by a special police officer and a marine, and four deaths of unknown parties which occurred in parts of the city not occupied by the regular army. No deaths occurred by action of the regular troops."

After the fire, though, the militia and the "specials" were guilty of hasty, arbitrary, and sometimes tragically stupid acts. The matter came to a head the night of April 22 when H. C. Tilden, a prominent San Franciscan and a member of the Mayor's Relief Committee, was shot and killed as he motored past a "citizen's" guard at the corner of Twenty-second and Guerrero.

The Woodmen of the World, for some reason, lost no time in setting up headquarters in Golden Gate Park. (*Bear Photo Service*)

With what appears to be grudging consent, these independent diners oblige the cameraman in Alamo Square. (*Bear Photo Service*)

The fact that the rifleman didn't see the Red Cross flag on the car didn't diminish the public indignation.

Of conflict between the regular police and the military, Police Chief Dinan said the reports were exaggerated. He did request that only regular army troops be permitted to patrol. One of Dinan's men was fired upon at Hayes and Van Ness on the twenty-fourth. "Fortunately all were poor marksmen," he reported later.

In spite of the difficulties, large and small, in which the troops became embroiled before their departure, San Franciscans generally viewed their work as a blessing. The bitter points were soon forgotten.

Arnold Genthe's "Stairs that Lead to Nowhere" recalls Gelett Burgess' words of love from "The Heart Line," published in 1907: "There it lay, a constellation of lights, a golden radiance, dimmed by the distance. San Francisco the Impossible, the City of Miracles! Of it and its people many stories have been told, and many shall be; but a thousand tales shall not exhaust its treasury of Romance. Earthquake and fire shall not change it, terror and suffering shall not break its glad, mad spirit." (California Palace of the Legion of Honor)

Lowell High School, at Sutter and Gough, served as temporary police headquarters in summer. Damage to schools prompted plan to open on double-shift basis. (California Historical Society)

Arnold Genthe protested, in his own words, against the "musclebound tradition of his day," and when he took this splendid shot, perhaps hiding the camera with his coat as he often did, he again demonstrated the ability to turn even the most commonplace scene into fine composition and superb human study. The view is at the corner of Bush and Fillmore, with St. Dominic's in the rear. (California Palace of the Legion of Honor)

Badly wrenched by the quake and propped by rails and timbers against future shock, the Turk and Fillmore car barns carried on until other facilities could be repaired. (California Historical Society)

As the days lengthened into summer, the problems of immediate relief gave way to those of long-range care. During the first days, perhaps 300,000 slept out of doors —the homeless plus the many who wouldn't sleep inside for fear of another quake. The number of campers in June, however, had dwindled to a fraction of this—less than 50,000. In July the number had dropped to 25,000, and in the fall of 1906, the permanent population of the camps amounted to little more than 17,000.

Bread lines were discontinued the first of August, and free food distribution was limited to the 20,000 still classed as "needy."

The makeshift shelters of blankets and rugs which helped shield two hundred thousand from the rain after the fire didn't last for long. Tents issued by the military replaced them, and the beginnings of the permanent camps which were to dot the City's parks and reservations for more than a year were established. The problem of housing a city in which three fifths of the

A pretty girl turned her back to the camera, and the photographer snapped a memorable shot. Another sidewalk kitchen is remembered for this slogan: "Eat, Drink and Be Merry, for Tomorrow We May Have to Go to Oakland." (Morton-Waters Company)

Red Cross official pauses in the Park to watch as photographer coaxes four sets of refugee twins to smile. (California Historical Society)

dwellings had burned was met in many ways. And in the final analysis, most of the people solved it for themselves.

Those who had any means or prospects did not have to rely on the good works of the committee for very long. Tens of thousands of San Franciscans, mostly women and children, were bundled off to spend the summer with friends or relatives while the struggle to rebuild the City was launched. Many thousands of others moved in with the fortunate San Franciscans whose homes had been spared.

Sailors stop to pose with the old miner who took it upon himself to keep a big pot of water hot in Golden Gate Park for weeks after the fire. In the upper picture, a young lad washes his hands in the steaming water from the siphon tap. In the lower picture, the water, the miner, and the camera are forgotten. (California Historical Society)

REFUGEES ATTENTION

Dr. Devine, "THE GEN-EROUS" and his allies, The Finance Committee, "THE NOBLE" will banquet on the fat of the land to-night with the relief funds which belong to us at the St. Francis Hotel, Tuesday night, July 31, 1906.

Meet, one and all, at Jefferson Square at 7 p. m. and march to the St. Francis Hotel, bearing the old clothes and soup as an emblem of their generosity to us.

Let the whole world know that while we are starving they are feasting. Such infamy was never known.

COME ONE - COME ALL

Good Speakers present

COMMITTEE OF FRIENDS OF REFUGEES

Not everyone was pleased with the work of the Committee. (Bancroft Library)

Mayor Schmitz's portrait helped these young hustlers sell cold drinks in the dry and dusty days after the fire. He was a hero then, but dark times were ahead. (Thomas C. Boyle)

Hot food stations, like this one in Union Square, served almost 1½ million meals from May to October in 1906. Interior shot of the same kitchen, below, shows the Spartan simplicity of the arrangement. Those who could afford it, about one out of a hundred, paid 15¢. The others were issued free tickets by the Red Cross. Here is a typical daily menu: BREAKFAST—Hash or Mush and Milk, Bread or Hot Biscuit, Coffee, and Sugar; DINNER—Soup, Roast Beef or Hash, Vegetable, Bread, Coffee, and Sugar; SUPPER—Soup or Irish Stew, Bread or Hot Biscuits, Tea, and Sugar. (Bear Photo Service; Bancroft Library)

This sweeping panorama, like the two on the opposite page, taken from a camera hoisted aloft by a string of kites. The Mint, center, is at the corner of Mission and Fifth streets. City Hall is at the far left.

In autumn the committee replaced the canvas shelters in the camps with two and three room wooden structures in anticipation of the winter rains. The committee called the little houses "cottages," but to this day the popular name "refugee shacks" has stuck. The Lands and Building Department, which was the sub-committee in charge of camps, built 6000 of the little houses in more than a dozen locations. The two-room "cottages" cost the committee $100 each and the three-roomers $150, including plumbing. As the pictures show, there was barely enough room to breathe in the permanent camps, but the committee did not view them as resorts, and made no apologies.

The camps were made up almost exclusively of working people—many of them from the South of Market

Aerial photography was quite an art in 1906. Airplanes could barely get off the ground then, and lighter-than-air ships were expensive and cumbersome. An enterprising midwesterner, George Lawrence, devised and patented this ingenious system of kites and wires, right, that carried a 46-pound panoramic camera 800 feet into the air. It was with this arrangement that these three pictures were taken. Lawrence and his local associate, Harry Myers, played out half a mile of line before the camera was at the proper altitude. When they were ready to shoot, they checked with binoculars to make sure the lens was lined up, and then tripped the shutter with an electrical impulse generated by an old style telephone magneto. A device within the camera then swept across a 90-degree arc to expose the image to a 22 by 55 inch negative. (Oakland Tribune)

RIGHT: *Lacking power to run, these cable cars stand idly on Sutter line. One cable line, California Street Railway, straightened twisted tracks, rebuilt the power house, and was back in business by August of 1906. (Automobile Manufacturers Association)* LEFT: *Life in the camps had much of the flavor of barracks life. Here a Jefferson Square kitchen hand looks up from his job—the traditional KP favorite, peeling spuds. (California Historical Society)* CENTER: *Mayor Schmitz reads the Declaration of Independence in Golden Gate Park on the Fourth of July following the fire. (Thomas C. Boyle)*

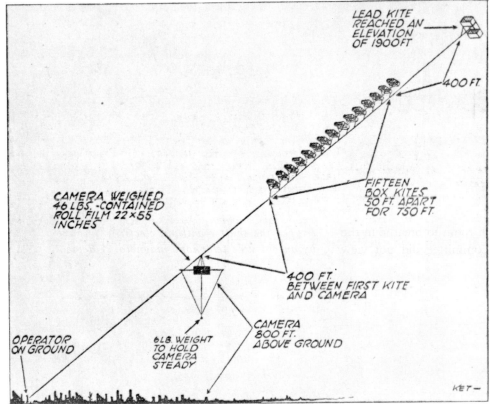

LEAD KITE REACHED AN ELEVATION OF 1900 FT

400 FT.

FIFTEEN BOX KITES 50 FT. APART FOR 750 FT.

CAMERA WEIGHED 46 LBS. -CONTAINED ROLL FILM 22×55 INCHES

400 FT. BETWEEN FIRST KITE AND CAMERA

6 LB. WEIGHT TO HOLD CAMERA STEADY

CAMERA 800 FT. ABOVE GROUND

OPERATOR ON GROUND

KET—

Opposite view looking over Nob Hill toward business district, South of the Slot, and the distant Mission. Fairmont Hotel, center, dwarfs the Call Building. City Hall and Ferry Building are easy to spot. (Panoramas courtesy of Harry Myers)

Three years after the pictures above were taken, a great part of the downtown section had been completely rebuilt. View here was shifted slightly to the east. Goat Island, far left. Mason Street cuts across right corner.

Harbor View Camp, with Alcatraz in the background, sheltered what was reputedly the toughest, most unmanageable group of refugees. The camp was run for many months by a remarkable 24-year-old physician, Dr. Rene Bine. (San Francisco Chamber of Commerce)

and Mission districts. The relief committee was firm in demanding proof of need before one of the cabins could be rented. One family, claiming to have been burnt out, arrived to apply for a three-room shack in one of the parks with *eight* wagonloads of household goods. Needless to say, they were turned away.

One of the prime considerations in jamming the homeless into small areas was that sanitary practices could be closely watched. The fear of epidemic hung over the head of the authorities for many months. About 12,000 people, mostly single men, lived outside the camps in improvised housing. The cottages were not available to them, on the grounds that they could earn enough' to provide their own quarters. Most cot-

tages were occupied by a family or by a widow with children.

The shanty dwellers constituted a much larger health problem than the camp dwellers. An outbreak of typhoid in September took $17,000 and much volunteer help to bring under control.

Life in the camps was simple. Each one was administered by an army officer—a "benevolent despot" who ruled with a strong hand. In the early weeks of camp life, the soldiers on duty were always armed, but as months rolled on, the need for such measures vanished in all but a couple of the tougher camps.

The committee charged the tenants $2 per month, but this money was put aside for the occupant in antici-

"Whence all but him had fled"

FRANCIS
Five days through fire and earthquake, without food, in the Hotel St. Francis wine cellars, San Francisco

One of the best known heroes of the fire was Francis, the wine steward's terrier who hid in the St. Francis wine cellars through the fire. He's shown here on a postcard. Francis was a noted celebrity for years, but few survivors remember him now. Another story circulated at the time told of a man trapped in a refrigerator at Palladini's Market on Clay when the quake jammed the door shut. According to the tale, he was found hopelessly insane when rescuers broke through after the fire. In another version two men, similarly trapped, were found frozen stiff. (St. Francis Hotel)

The blaze at the corner of Twenty-second Street and Mission was one of the biggest put out by the firemen on the morning of the eighteenth. It took six engines, using water found two blocks away, more than fours hours to keep the flames from burning more than the large corner area shown here.
(*Society of California Pioneers*)

pation of the day when he could move the cottage to a private lot. It was part of the original plan that the cottages eventually would be moved to the refugee's own location.

The camps were crowded, all right, but the settings of several, particularly the three in Golden Gate Park, were so pleasant that Mayor Schmitz was prompted to say, "I'm only afraid these people will never want to leave their new homes here." Running water, efficient sewers, bath houses, fire protection, and good drainage were all provided in each camp.

The general health of the City was vastly improved in the months following the fire compared to what it had been before. Several factors were at work here, of course. Many of the sickly and dissipated left town. The fresh air that all were getting in large quantities no doubt had a good effect. Liquor was banned, and despite hardship for some, this undoubtedly had a good effect, too. The health and good conduct of the population in the sixty days following the fire would have been hard to match anywhere in the world.

As the months grew on, there were little notes of dis-

Arnold Genthe's view of hot meal kitchen on outer Market Street. Unmistakable silhouette of City Hall, center, Call Building, distant right. Gloom which hangs over the top of picture is due to a faulty negative. (California Palace of the Legion of Honor)

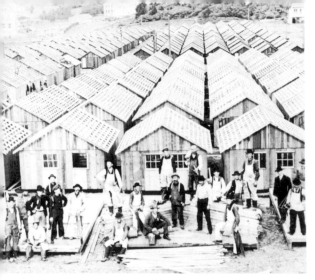

These views are typical of the 5600 cottages built in camps throughout the City. Building is in progress, left, along what is now Park Presidio Drive, with the Marine Hospital in the background. Mission Park is shown right, and below is Lobos Square Camp, now called Funston Playground. (California Historical Society)

cord in the camps—dissatisfaction with the relief committee, and inevitable friction between neighbors. Some spoke gloomily of camp life and its effect on the family. Wrote one lady journalist, "Mothers drink, young girls have drifted into immoral lives, and children are growing used to uncontrolled uselessness."

The next reporter, however, might have commented on the cheery, healthy appearance of the refugees and the good the experience had done the working classes.

The truth is, life went on much as usual, with the refugees making the best of it with all the rest. No one claimed that a refugee camp was the end of a rainbow or that the people who lived in them were saintly.

Signs adorn the ragged front of the Jackson brewery on Folsom near Eleventh. One of the signs reads: "CALIFORNIA BAKING CO. *Eddy and Fillmore Sts.* SAVED *the City with* BREAD *without light or power. Bakery run day and night. Supplies* EVERYBODY NOW. *Chas. Loesch, Mgr.*" *Even ruined churches were plastered with ads after the fire. (California Historical Society)*

From the beginning, there were agitators who condemned the whole relief program. Driven by a variety of motives, they attracted a following which nettled the relief leaders to the point of exasperation. The agitators stirred up enough fuss that it came to the attention of the nation as a whole. Their specific complaints may or may not have had a reasonable basis, but it's obvious the relief administrators did their very best to act fairly and quickly with the funds they had.

Eventually, it all blew over. Starting toward the end of summer in 1907, the cottages were moved to the owners' own lots. Workmen jacked the buildings up off their simple foundations, set them on wheels, and with horses or mules supplying the power, hauled them to the new homesites. Many still stand, often unrecognizable, in scattered sections through the City.

For all the hardship the people of the South of Market and Mission districts had to endure, the long-range gain for many of them surely outweighed the privation. Relief plans were aimed at making a home owner, rather than a renter, out of the workingman. Refugee shacks were in many cases the first homes ever owned by their occupants.

The relocation of the cottages was only a beginning. The Housing and Shelter Committee, under the direction of Father D. O. Crowley, spent $600,000 building 1400 houses for persons who could match the amount spent by the committee. These houses were not restricted to the burned area as were those for which the Lands and Building Department provided funds. This group, headed by Thomas McGee, offered a bonus to former home owners, regardless of means, amounting up to one-third the cost of the house if the house was built in the burned area. The half million so spent speeded the healing of the awful scar left by the fire. Many thousands took advantage of the "bonus."

The Department of Relief and Rehabilitation was the largest of all the Red Cross subcommittees. Headed by F. W. Dohrmann, this group gave away $3,020,000 for individual relief. More than 28,500 applications for funds passed through the committee's hands.

The grants ranged from $20 to $300, with the average grant amounting to about $100. The Department covered many needs. It found homes for orphan and unwanted children, bought sewing machines (1600 of them at a cost of $36,000) so that mothers could begin to fashion new wardrobes for their families, made cash grants to unsupported and partially supported families, bought furniture for those who had nothing left, and took care of the aged. No one in want was turned away unless another committee could serve him better.

The Three Traitors!

DEVINE, PHELAN AND POLLOCK

We, the refugees and citizens of San Francisco, denounce these men as traitors to their trust. The law says that any guardian or trustees of funds or property belonging to any person or persons by heirship or gift, or by any other acquisition, who shall unlawfully or negligently misapply or wantonly waste, destroy or otherwise keep from the ward or person or persons to whom it lawfully belongs, or the person or persons who are to be benefited thereby, is guilty of misdemeanor and liable to punishment for such breach of trust, according to the laws in such cases made and provided.

Now, whereas the above named Devine, Phelan and Pollock and their associates have been recreant to their duty in handling the Red Cross funds placed in their hands as trustees by the donors thereof as a gift of the people of the United States to the refugees and sufferers caused by the earthquake and fire which destroyed our city, by withholding and keeping from them that which was intended to be used for their benefit, and by otherwise squandering for automobiles, large salaries and other needless expenditures, speculating in flour and other goods, large amounts of funds in their hands, and by neglecting or refusing to pay their obligations, have worked a great hardship upon the beneficiaries thereof and have been traitors to their trust, and deserve the condemnation and contempt of all honest people.

We therefore pray that President Roosevelt, Secretary of War Taft and Mr. Magee of the Red Cross Society, immediately take action to remove Dr. Devine from our State, thus saving the citizens from the odious duty of persuading him to retire at once. We also pray that Messrs. Phelan and Pollock will also retire from the Finance Committee and save the indignant people from over-indulgence in the use of tar and feathers.

Gen. Greely says we are a lot of paupers. The Finance Committee is attempting to form another grafting corporation to build houses for the refugees.

Signed, sealed and delivered by the Committee of the Whole.

People of San Francisco

Three leaders of the relief forces came under the attack of malcontents. Underlying this and similar broadsides was the belief that relief money should have been distributed to the people and that relief officials were engaged in underhanded financial deals with relief funds. (Bancroft Library)

Demonstrations of this sort were held frequently, but little was accomplished. Most refugees were unsympathetic toward the agitators. (Bear Photo Service)

Fire occasionally broke out in the cottage camps, but unlike the big fire that was the cause for the shacks in the first place, all were quickly brought under control. (Society of California Pioneers)

Members of the Odorless Excavator team, which emptied latrines, pose with their mules in Golden Gate Park. (Society of California Pioneers)

The stables out in the Ingleside race track were converted by Relief and Rehabilitation people to house the city's aged and infirmed. Floors were installed and hot and cold water was piped in to make cozy, white-washed apartments for about 1000 guests. Some of the stables were reserved for the old ladies, some for the old gents, and others for married couples. Others were converted for such things as a chapel, a butcher's shop, a dining hall, a laundry, and a hospital. It was a self-sufficient settlement—almost.

For those who couldn't work, little comforts were not forgotten—tobacco was rationed out each Wednesday to the old men, and there was a sewing room with six machines for the ladies. Everything—lodging, food, medical care—came to about $250,000 for the year and a half the stables were in operation—not quite $14 a month per person.

One group of relief workers—the women in charge of aid to destitute families—had a heart-rending job. Often the problem involved a sick or worthless husband. But the depressing repetition of sad tales was broken sometimes. One of the humorous stories to come out of their work involved a Swedish lady whose three strong sons built her a little house to replace the one taken by the fire. It wasn't until the new house was finished that they found they had built on the wrong lot.

Stables at the Ingleside race track were converted for the City's old folks. Although the quarters still looked like stables, as does the ladies' hospital ward shown here, it was a comfortable solution to what might have been a very difficult problem. (Bear Photo Service)

128

Many couldn't qualify for camp cottages, or refused to accept the restrictions of camp life and chose instead to live in ramshackle huts in the post-fire era. Because sanitation was difficult to control outside the camps, shantytowns such as this were frowned on.
(Bear Photo Service)

The committee on business rehabilitation had $500,000 to spend. Almost all of the applicants were self-employed men and women whose only means of livelihood had been destroyed. Some were boarding-house keepers and some were barbers. Grocers, tailors, restaurateurs, printers, hucksters, bootmakers, and milliners were helped with small grants. There was even a Chinese cigarmaker in the list. Almost nine hundred people in scores of common and not-so-common trades and businesses were given aid. The average grant— about $250—doesn't seem like much today, but it was enough then to open cigar stands and sheet-metal shops.

Life went on in the shattered city much as life goes on any time, anywhere. People ate, slept, laughed, complained, cried, hoped and dreamed, and sometimes, forgetting the hurried business of the hour, rose to small, sublime moments of generosity and love.

San Francisco was happy and healthy, and it was with the vigor of youth that she turned to the task of rebuilding.

Camp life ended in the Summer of 1908. Most of the cottages had been transported to owners' lots, hauled in one piece by teams of horses. This cottage, which may still stand somewhere in San Francisco, is on its way from Lobos Square Camp. Notice the legs of two small boys who are pushing the cabin from behind.
(California Historical Society)

ERECTED to the GLORY of GOD and in LOV MEM

Stanford Memorial Church
April 20, 1906
(Berton Crandall Collection)

SWATH
OF
DESTRUCTION

Workmen pause on the third floor of Santa Rosa's County Courthouse during cleanup. Cupola stood several stories higher before the quake.

To the North

No American city was ever hit harder by an earthquake than Santa Rosa was in 1906. The quiet seat of Sonoma County, set in the midst of some of California's loveliest country, was struck by a walloping force that toppled almost every brick building in the downtown section.

At 5 A.M. that chilly morning, the April eighteenth issue of the Santa Rosa *Press Democrat* was off the presses, and the printers were winding up their day. Several of the delivery boys had arrived and were folding their papers when the quake hit. Three of them were smothered by cascading walls, but a fourth was later dragged alive from the ruins. Incidents like this

were common throughout the city, and when the last body was recovered, Santa Rosa counted more than seventy-five dead.

As in San Francisco, the pall of plaster dust hadn't even settled before blazes broke out. By luck, the firehouse hadn't been damaged badly, and two steam en-

The Press Democrat

VOL. XXXII   SANTA ROSA, CAL., APRIL 19, 1906.   NO. 93

A DREADFUL CATASTROPHE VISITS SANTA ROSA

A frightful disaster overtook Santa Rosa yesterday. Just as the dawn was breaking, a mighty earthquake struck the city. It came with awful force and suddenness, hurling many people from their beds. Before the terrified community could realize what had happened, the entire business section was a mass of ruins, every residence had been more or less damaged, some being completely wrecked, and approximately half a hundred or more people had been swept into eternity. Flames immediately broke out in all directions and lent additional horror to the scene.

List of Known Dead

N. L. Jones, manager Sunset Telephone Company.
Mrs. N. L. Jones, wife of the above.
Louis Blum, proprietor Sample Rooms, not recovered.
Mr. Greenwood, a commercial traveler, Hotel St. Rose.
John Baylor, Jr., proprietor of Capitol Saloon.
John Baylor Ter, son of the above.
Milo S. Fish, Pressman Press Democrat.
George Bluth, carrier Press Democrat.
Willie Bluth, carrier Press Democrat.
Charles Shepard, carrier Press Democrat.
F. W. Carter, jeweler, Fourth street.
Mrs. F. W. Carter, wife of the above.
Wayne Day, Palm Garden saloon.
Mrs. De Young and two children, Anderson valley, Mendocino Co.
Mrs. G. F. Manning, wife proprietor Grand Hotel.
Baby Manning, daughter of above.
Fred Schieffer, lineman Santa Rosa Lighting Co.
Miss Green, stewardess Hotel St. Rose.

William Peacock, contractor, San Francisco.
Mrs. William Peacock, wife of the above.
Eli Loeb, merchant, Third Street.
Mrs. H. H. Moke, wife of undertaker.
Miss Louise Moke, daughter of the above.
Miss Willie Reid, school teacher.
W. H. Mallory, of Vallejo.
S. H. Look, proprietor Look's Shoe Store.
Mr. Murphy, commercial traveler.
Child by the name of Kayser.
F. Harry Newman, druggist.
E. M. Pedigo, real estate agent.
N. K. Wescott, father of Mrs. Speegle.
Joe Woods, hop buyer.
Joseph Domenico, proprietor of the Western Hotel.
Truman McCord, barkeeper.
F. Dowling, employe City Stables.
Mrs. Ely, Grand Hotel.
Marshall Ely, son of the above.
Smith Davidson, capitalist.
Fritz Tanner from Eagle Hotel.
Biu Yuin, Chinese.
Mr. Bayes.
J. Bratker.
O G Slampli
C. Trudgeon, with M. H. Dignan
Miss Excelsa, Novelty theatre

A Miraculous Escape

After being beneath the ruins of the Eagle Hotel all day, Ferdinand Drey was taken out late last night uninjured.

San Jose is in Ruins

San Jose, Apr. 19—This city is in ruins. The beautiful St. James Hotel is totally destroyed. The annex of the Vendmore Hotel is wrecked.

Along First street, the principal business thoroughfare of the city, for a distance of several blocks there are not five buildings that have not been ruined. The Hall of Records and Court House are among those wrecked.

Ukiah Sends Provisions

A carload of provisions for distribution by the Relief Committee were sent here this morning by the citizens of Ukiah, headed by Mayor Weldon.

Holding the Inquests

Coroner Blackburn is holding the inquests over the remains of the unfortunate victims this morning in the lecture hall of the Christian Church.

Petaluma's Great Kindness

Petaluma proved the friend indeed to Santa Rosa on Wednesday. Her Elks Lodge sent a carload of provisions; the Chamber of Commerce did likewise. The physicians lent valuable assistance. So did Company C commanded by Captain Dickson. Kind sympathy and help came from everybody in our sister city.

Declared Legal Holiday

Governor Pardee last night declared today (Thursday) a legal holiday on account of the awful catastrophe.

Dead at Guerneville

Three men employed in the Great Eastern quicksilver mine at Guerneville were crushed to death by a falling rock during the earthquake on Wednesday morning.

Sacramento Damaged

Reports received in San Francisco say that great damage was done in Sacramento, the State Capitol and other public buildings being wrecked, and many residences having collapsed.

Harry Newman's Funeral

The funeral of the late Harry Newman will take place at 2 o'clock this afternoon from the Episcopal church. All members of Santa Rosa Elks Lodge are asked to attend.

News of San Francisco was sketchy, didn't make front page in this April 19 emergency edition of the local paper.

Townspeople claw through the wreckage of Press Democrat *offices. The paper above was printed on a borrowed press. Several were killed beneath these walls, but body claiming had to wait until fire passed over. Faulty construction, rather than earthquake intensity, was blamed for most of Santa Rosa's damage, but this was little consolation to the survivors.*
(California Historical Society)

132

gines were hurried into action to keep the fires from destroying what remained. The smaller town of Sebastopol, in the apple country to the west, sent its only engine to help in the battle. The three "steamers" fought together through the day. One man, buried deep in the rubble and half choked by the dust, lived to tell of the glorious sensation he felt when cool water pumped from the engines trickled down through the wreckage and across his face.

Once the fires were extinguished (and this wasn't until a large part of the hardest hit section had burned over), news began to filter in from the south. Only after refugees from San Francisco began to arrive did the townspeople understand the extent of the calamity. The April nineteenth edition of the *Press Democrat,* handset and run off a small job press at the Santa Rosa Business College, carried the story of Sacramento's supposed destruction on the front page, while only a small paragraph on the reverse side mentioned the fire in San Francisco. The first accurate report from the city to reach Santa Rosa newspaper readers ran in the April twenty-first edition of the *Democrat-Republican*—which was the unlikely title of an 8- by-10-inch sheet published by the two local papers for about three weeks.

Military lines were established in Santa Rosa after a team from Mare Island Navy Yard arrived to help recover bodies. The people of Santa Rosa set about cleaning up the mess with the same vigor and good spirit that marked San Francisco's recovery.

An editorial in the *Democrat-Republican* expressed the town's outlook without mincing:

"The one saving feature of the situation is that 'we are all in the same boat.' As a result of the complete destruction of the city's business interests, no man has any advantage over his neighbor. To put it frankly, we are all broke, and the moment anybody asks us to liquidate, 'the jig is up.' It is only by standing shoulder to shoulder for the rehabilitation of Santa Rosa, and showing our faith in the future and confidence in each other, that the great problem which now confronts this community can possibly be worked out. We will pay when we can."

Actually, Santa Rosa was about twenty miles from the fault line—a distance as great or greater than that between other comparable towns that suffered only minor damage. A number of theories were advanced to explain this, but the most reasonable puts the blame at the door of Santa Rosans themselves. Almost every brick building in the town had been put together with a lime mortar made of poor sand. Little attention had been paid to the need for adequate cross bracing, cross walls,

Men rushed to retrieve the injured, then property, on the morning of the eighteenth, as fire threatened to engulf what little was left of Santa Rosa. (California Historical Society)

Grim sign hangs on the ruined Santa Rosa City Hall doors reflecting the town's first concern—her dead and wounded. Below, City functionaries wait with salvaged records. (California Historical Society)

Earthquake damage hurt a far greater proportion of the people in Santa Rosa than in any other city or town. Eight to ten thousand would have been killed in San Francisco if the ratios had been the same.
(California Historical Society)

and proper anchoring of walls to floor and roof. Buildings as poorly constructed in San Francisco also went down in the shake.

Regardless of the cause, the Santa Rosans wasted no time in rebuilding. Only $40,000 in relief was needed, and every able-bodied man turned to the immediate task. One writer recalled, "Manual labor was the only recognized profession."

Although there was no lack of pride in the speed and spunk with which the town rebuilt, Santa Rosa seems more than any other damaged town to have minimized that page in her annals. In a fat history of Sonoma County published in 1937, for example, only two slight references to the quake are made, and it takes a bit of searching to find them.

Along the fault to the west a number of smaller towns and hamlets took the crushing brunt of the earthquake's power. Healdsburg, Sebastopol, Bloomfield, Tomales, Point Reyes, Olema, Fort Ross, to name just a few, were badly hit. Tomales, which was then a thriving and prosperous town, was more severely damaged than any other in Marin County. Two deaths were recorded there. A false report told of a great tidal wave which swept into Tomales Bay and completely de-

The church at Fort Ross, marking the southernmost penetration of the Russians before the Gold Rush, was thrown down violently by the tremor. The building has since been restored as a state historical monument.
(Branner Library)

The Catholic church at Tomales was devasted by the power of the quake. The church was never rebuilt. (Branner Library)

The earthquake pitched the hotel at Marshall into Tomales Bay, leaving the second floor at ground level. (Branner Library)

stroyed the towns of Tomales, Olema, Bolinas, and Inverness. A fisherman did report, however, a wave which swept into that long narrow bay, but although it looked a mile high as it came toward him, he later said it couldn't have been more than a ten-foot swell.

Fort Bragg, a lumber port on the coast to the north, was badly shaken by the quake and then swept by fire. The blaze didn't cover a large area, but a good part of the business section was taken. Far to the north, Eureka staggered under the quake's intensity and suffered as much damage as many towns close to the epicenter.

Most of the Sacramento Valley was awakened by the quake, although with isolated exceptions, no severe damage was done. Oscar Lewis remembers that morning vividly. He was in the pressroom of the Red Bluff newspaper, folding papers at the moment of the earthquake. The first hint came as the unshaded light hanging on a cord from the ceiling began to swing in an arc. He and the other newsboy with him ran from the building in time to see the façade of the City Hall fall into the street. The next day he and the other lad made a boy's fortune selling every paper the press could crank out to news-hungry refugees who poured through the town on special trains.

Fort Bragg sits far to the north of most of the damaged region, but earthquake and fire took their toll there, too. The Union Lumber Co. Mill, shown here, was left a shambles after the quake toppled a giant brick stack. (Stanford Collection)

Engineer William King and a young girl stand beside the prostrate train at Point Reyes Station. Somehow not a pane of glass was broken in the fall. (*Roy D. Graves Collection*)

To the East

The sparing of Oakland and Berkeley must be remembered as one of the great blessings of the quake. Without these and the East Bay's smaller towns, the plight of San Francisco's sufferers would have been infinitely worse. As it was, the homes and institutions of California's third and fourth largest cities were ready and able to help.

No deaths were reported in either Berkeley or Ala-

In Oakland, five were killed in the upstairs rooms when wall of adjoining building fell in the Empire Theatre. (*Oakland* Tribune)

meda, and the actual damage was light in those two towns. In Oakland, five were killed when the wall of a building fell through the ceiling of an apartment above a theater on Twelfth Street. Chimneys were down all over, and at scattered points, building fronts were thrown out, steeples fell over, and houses were thrown from their foundations. One small fire started in Oakland, but it was quickly smothered. The water system had not been damaged.

Relief camps were set up in a number of spots throughout the city, including a large camp for Chinese refugees at Eighth and Ninth streets near Lake Merritt. In the first days, almost 50,000 refugees were quartered in Oakland, but within a few weeks, many went back to San Francisco. The remaining non-Chinese campers were finally settled at Adams Point on the lake. The Chinese, here as in San Francisco, took assistance only as long as it was absolutely necessary.

At the Emeryville race track near Shellmound Park a highly specialized relief camp went into operation the first day. The *Examiner* reported on the twenty-third that "Johnny Lyons, a bookmaker, drew $7000 from one of the San Francisco banks while the fire was raging and has provided living expenses for many a track follower left penniless."

Business in Oakland took only one day off, then carried on as if nothing had happened. Prices were not hiked, but the pace quickened. A few tried to capitalize on fear, like the real estate man who advertised on April 18 in the Oakland *Herald:*

136

The pole above Oakland's City Hall was whipped into an arc by the quake, but building stands solid. Many refugees wait in line to register. Militia camps on lawn. (Bancroft Library)

Shock stripped upper wall from this building on Washington Street near Twelfth in Oakland. Considering damage elsewhere, the town escaped relatively unscathed. (Oakland Tribune)

MANY PEOPLE
KILLED

in flats and rooming houses, but none in the suburbs. I have several new cottages in East Oakland and Fruitvale from $950 to $3000, small payment down, balance like rent.

M. T. MINNEY
470 11th St.

Far more characteristic was the subdued note of this three-column department store ad:

TAFT AND PENNOYER
WILL BE OPEN AS USUAL
TOMORROW MORNING

Any number of San Francisco businesses relocated temporarily in Oakland, and for a while the town had the look of a frontier mining settlement. It reminded one writer of, ". . . Cripple Creek or Leadville in the days of a boom, save that horsemen and rowdies are absent."

If anyone desires physical evidence of Oakland's role after the earthquake, he should take a look at the 1907 city directory—it's twice the size of the 1906 edition. Oakland served as a great backstop, a reservoir of

Oakland's First Baptist Church was so badly shaken by the quake that it had to be torn down. Here onlookers run across Telegraph Avenue as the winch-pulled lines tear the steeple off the main structure. Lines which pulled the steeple loose lie in the street, bottom center. (Morton-Waters Company)

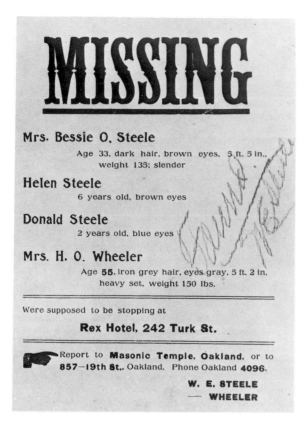

Handbills advertising for lost relatives and friends were tacked up all over. This one tells its own story. (Californiana Collection, San Jose Library)

Saddest scene of the entire tragedy was the State Hospital for the Insane at Agnew, near San Jose. Tiny figures, right, search through debris of women's ward. (T. T. Tourtillott)

Wednesday's paper in San Jose published before news of the disaster in San Francisco had reached that far south. Out-of-state news was set in type before quake hit.

strength, for the City during the rebuilding. As the San Francisco *Examiner* said in the week following the quake, "Never can San Francisco forget the nobility of Oakland." And exactly the same could have been said for Berkeley and the smaller towns of the East Bay, whose work in relief was smaller only in proportion to their size.

To the South

If you picture Santa Rosa as the hub of destruction north of San Francisco, consider San Jose as the focal point to the south. When the fury of the earth hit that old California city, walls and buildings collapsed to produce some of the most spectacular wreckage of the earthquake.

The new Hall of Justice, many churches, a hotel an-

General view of the wrecked Agnew's Asylum. After three days of digging through ruins, the exhausted workers thought they had reclaimed the last body. Then a voice was heard crying, "Never mind me, get the others first." Frantically, they dug toward the sound as the voice repeated the cry. When the patient was hauled to safety, the rescuers considered it a miracle. That is, until they learned he had escaped from the keeper only an hour before and had hidden himself in the debris. (T. T. Tourtillott)

Water tanks withstood the shock, while the rigid, poorly tied together buildings at Agnew's failed to hold. (T. T. Tourtillott)

In San Jose, many large buildings collapsed in the shock. Here, the main part of Saint Patrick's lies in the street. (T. T. Tourtillott)

nex, and several large business buildings stood as shells or collapsed specters of their original splendor. Frame houses in all parts of town slipped off their foundations, and although the death toll was mercifully low, 8000 people were left homeless. Nineteen were reported dead.

But of all the tragic scenes the earthquake left anywhere along its two hundred-mile trail, none was sadder than that at Agnew's state hospital for the insane, just a few miles to the north.

There a stern, four-story brick structure which housed more than 1000 inmates dominated a cluster of lesser outbuildings. More than a hundred inmates and a dozen keepers perished under the falling walls at the time of the quake. Pandemonium broke loose, but although rumors spread through the South Bay Area that hundreds of insane were roaming the countryside, no serious incident was ever reported.

Young men and priests from Santa Clara University were among the first to reach the spot. Most of them ran all the way. It was a grisly scene. The mangled bodies of some had already been dragged from the ruins by survivors, and hundreds of the inmates wailed and cried

Like a great doll's house, the Home Union Building stands stripped to the view. Note party decorations, upper right. (California Historical Society)

Balcony of the Unique Theatre might have been a scene of chaos if the quake had struck a few hours earlier. (California Historical Society)

"bloody murder," as one of the young students, now Father Ernest Watson, noted. Some of the more violent patients had to be strapped to trees with sheets and blankets to keep them from harming others. One kept calling, "Jesus of Nazareth is passing."

All during that day and the day following, wagons moved in a steady procession to San Jose carrying the dead and wounded. The final death count: 119.

In downtown San Jose, fire had broken out in two places. It was an all-day battle for the local department to bring them under control. The militia was called out early in the day, and a large part of the downtown section was roped off. Mayor Worswick issued a warning that crimes and misdemeanors would be punished with "a heavy hand." San Jose was San Francisco in miniature that day.

Curious lad stares back as cameraman shoots collapsed Mayer Bros.' clothing store on Santa Clara Street. (California Historical Society)

Fortunately, San Jose was spared both the numbing devastation by earthquake that crushed Santa Rosa and the ravage of conflagration that leveled most of San Francisco.

The problem of getting news from the outside was bad, but no worse in San Jose than in other towns in the earthquake region. The *Evening News* printed this roundup before noon on the eighteenth:

"The following reports were circulated at ten o'clock: Stanford University buildings badly wrecked, with heavy loss of life.

Santa Cruz badly shaken, loss of life heavy; all important buildings destroyed.

No trains from north or south had arrived at 10 o'clock.

The wires being down the reports could not be verified.

Local trains were started from San Jose to San Francisco, with instructions to proceed as far as possible.

11 A.M.—A man is reported to have arrived from San Francisco, in an auto, reporting that the disaster there is worse than in San Jose.

Late—Thousands of people reported killed in San Francisco."

The report of Santa Cruz' destruction was the product of someone's imagination, but Stanford University, to the north of San Jose, was indeed badly wrecked.

A whole string of towns which lie between San Jose and San Francisco and southward from San Jose to Salinas suffered major damage. Of those to the south, San Juan Bautista, Hollister, and Gilroy were struck

The quake buried a score beneath the fallen walls of the Vendome Hotel Annex at First and Hobsen streets in San Jose. All but one man were rescued. (California Historical Society)

Proclamation !

In view of the great calamity that has befallen us, and for the better police and fire protection of the city, and for the better security of life and property, I hereby recommend that all the people remain at their homes during the coming night, from and after the hour of 7:30 p.m. of this day, and I do hereby command that all persons, save and except only those who have especial business to transact therein, and permission so to do, remain away from that part of the business section of the city now being especially patrolled.

ALL LAWLESSNESS WILL BE REPRESSED WITH A HEAVY HAND

The co-operation of all good citizens is invoked in aid of the enforcement of this Order.

G. D. WORSWICK
Mayor.

San Jose, Cal., April 18, 1906.

Mayor Worswick issued a temperate proclamation on the day of the tragedy, and in spite of severe earthquake damage and two stubborn fires the town remained well behaved. But a man named Coykendall insisted that a vigilance committee should be formed, and he spent most of the morning trying to round up support. No one was interested. So out of sheer frustration, he had posters printed, below, and tacked them up on poles and fences in the downtown section that afternoon. Nobody paid any attention except to tear them down as souvenirs of an otherwise sobering day.

WARNING!

●●●●●●●●●●●●●●●●●●●●●●●●●●●●●●●●●●●●●●●

NOTICE IS GIVEN that any person found Pilfering, Stealing, Robbing, or committing any act of Lawless Violence will be summarily

HANGED

●●●●●●●●●●●●●●●●●●●●●●●●●●●●●●●●●●●●●●●

Vigilance Committee.

Children were excused from school for a few days in San Jose, but as soon as simple shelter could be rigged up, they were called back. Kids treated the whole affair as an adventure. (Californiana Collection, San Jose Library)

Hand-set newspaper tells a remarkably good story of the destruction, considering the situation. Paper's claim to be the first printed in earthquake zone is probably true.

hardest. Near Salinas, the huge six-story Spreckels sugar mill with acres of floor space was left a half-ruined shell. Built on filled ground near the Salinas River, the mill took a worse beating than any other steel structure in the state.

Farther to the south, beyond the end of the visible break, the little town of Priest Valley was shaken badly. And hundreds of miles farther south, the railroad town of Brawley in the Imperial Valley was smashed by the earthquake. Its five hundred inhabitants were awakened by the same violence that shook a million Northern Californians. Why brick and adobe walls should have been thrown down in Brawley while Alcatraz Island—only a mile from San Francisco—slept through the quake has never been adequately explained.

To the north of San Jose, a dozen small towns shuddered in unison on the morning of the eighteenth and their main streets had a familiar look about them. Santa Clara, Sunnyvale, Mountain View, Palo Alto, Menlo Park, Redwood City and San Mateo all saw prominent buildings collapse. On the Coast side, towns like Half Moon Bay were similarly visited.

Of the cities, Palo Alto was the most severely hurt. Almost every business building was damaged. To the north, just over the Menlo Park line, St. Patrick's Seminary, said at the time to be the nation's most beautiful, was wrecked. By some "miracle," as it was said, no one was hurt.

But at Stanford, fate had not been so kind.

Leland Stanford Junior University was only fifteen years old in 1906. It was built with the millions of Senator Leland Stanford, one of the swashbucklers who drove the Central Pacific across the Sierras in the 1860s to link San Francisco with the East. Stanford's life was marked by a tragedy that power and wealth could not soften. His only son, Leland Stanford, Jr., died of fever in Rome—a promising boy of fifteen years. The grief-ridden mother and father dedicated what was left of their lives to the building of a university in his name.

The central buildings, which formed a quadrangle focused on a large and ornate church. It had already attracted world attention. The beautiful mosaic front was a masterpiece of modern Venetian artistry, although there were those who objected to the size and wording of the dedicatory message which ran across the front: "Erected to the Glory of God and in Loving Memory of My Husband Leland Stanford."

Gilroy, like other small towns of the Santa Clara Valley and Peninsula, was well punished by the temblor. (Branner Library)

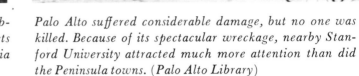

One man was killed and several were injured when Hobson's Clothing Store, at the corner of First and Post streets in San Jose, collapsed like a folding chair. (California Historical Society)

Palo Alto suffered considerable damage, but no one was killed. Because of its spectacular wreckage, nearby Stanford University attracted much more attention than did the Peninsula towns. (Palo Alto Library)

Looking toward the east on University Avenue in Palo Alto. The town, though badly damaged, quickly organized for the expected horde of refugees from San Francisco. Philosopher William James, at Stanford at the time, found the completeness of Palo Alto's organization almost comical, since only a handful of refugees came to Palo Alto. Of his experience in the critical period, James said, "I heard not a single really pathetic or sentimental word expressed by anyone." (Berton Crandall Collection)

This universally circulated view symbolized the earthquake tragedy for many. The broken "Angel of Grief" knelt by tomb of Jane Stanford's brother on Stanford campus. (Berton Crandall Collection)

Interior of the Stanford Memorial Church was left a ruin when the clock tower crashed through the roof. Beautiful mosaics, statuary, stone carvings were world renowned. (Berton Crandall Collection)

Massive sandstone gates at the entrance to Stanford University stood on El Camino Real, trail of the Mission Fathers.

Great arch at entrance to the Quad was a prominent ruin. (Berton Crandall Collection)

On the morning of the eighteenth much of their work stood in ruins. The chimneys of Encina Hall, the freshmen men's dormitory, fell in, forming light wells where none had been before. Many were trapped—either by falling wreckage or by jammed doors. The new library and gymnasium were complete wrecks. Many of the graceful arches which supported the dark esplanades that ring the "Quad" were set askew and in the center of it all, the church stood in shambles. The mosaic front had been blown off the front by the air pressure built up when the clock tower crashed through the roof. The church was later taken down and rebuilt from scratch. "The ruin is simply appalling," said the Palo Alto *Tribune* that day.

The early hour of the quake was a blessing almost everywhere. At places like Agnew's Asylum, it didn't make any difference, but at Stanford it meant the difference between mere damage to the buildings and a human tragedy unmatched in American history. As it was, two were killed—a freshman at Encina Hall, and a maintenance man who was crushed by a falling stack. What the scene might have been on a Sunday morning with the church jammed with worshipers is frightening to imagine.

Teddy Roosevelt wired David Starr Jordan, president of the University. ". . . . I most earnestly hope

Gates shown above were thrown down by the shock. Stanford ruins were greatly publicized in earthquake literature. (Berton Crandall Collection)

Stones in the foreground were numbered while the Stanford Church was dismantled. After steel frame was built, church was pieced back together. Tower clock and chimes were placed in a "temporary" tower behind the church, where they have remained, marking the hours, to this day. (Berton Crandall Collection)

that things are not as bad as they are reported." But they were, almost. No set of buildings, save those in Santa Rosa and at Agnew's, was so devastated by the quake.

Dr. Jordan voiced the Stanford attitude the first day when he said, "It is only an incident in the day's work, and does not change the development of the institution in the slightest degree."

Out West, one of several magazines devoted to the Far West and its fortunes said, "Fancy an Eastern university losing $5 million by a natural convulsion before breakfast; and by lunch-time arranging its next year on a larger scale than ever!"

The school might have been a youngster, but the quake provided it with a rich history—a tradition. It was a mark of pride. As a writer in the *Overland Monthly* commented, "Nothing infuriated the . . . survivors more than the placid and unruffled relatives who calmly wrote: 'How dreadful about San Francisco. I'm glad you were too far away to feel the shock.'"

Statue of Louis Agassiz toppled from its perch on the Stanford quadrangle during the quake and broke through the pavement. The sight prompted quips such as, ". . . the headforemost scientist in the U.S." and ". . . a fine fellow in the abstract, but no good in the concrete." (Stanford Collection)

Brand new gymnasium, left, and domed library down the road were demolished by the earthquake. Southeast corner of Quad is visible on the far right. No buildings stand on these two sites today. (Berton Crandall Collection)

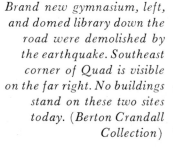

Earth slip along San Francisco's Union Street west of Steiner. (California Palace of the Legion of Honor)

ROCKS AND HISTORY

Surface rupture at the head of Tomales Bay. The earth's crust broke and shifted for hundreds of miles along the rift. Horizontal displacement reached a maximum of 21 feet in this region. The western side, left, moved northward, the eastern side, southward. Some geologists believe that rocks on western side match rocks 300 miles to the south on the eastern side. The furrowing shown in the picture is a result of an earthquake-producing break in rocks far below the surface. (Branner Library)

Landslide in a redwood forest dammed Los Gatos Creek. (Branner Library)

Tracks bulged where fault crossed tracks near Santa Cruz. Two tunnels collapsed on this road. (Branner Library)

As ONE might suspect, very little time passed before a rash of theories spilled forth in the journals of the day to explain the origin of the earthquake.

"God rules in the storm, the volcanic eruption, the tidal wave, and the earthquake," said the editor of *The New World,* a Roman Catholic journal. "He is the Lord and Master of nature and its laws, as well as of the supernatural sphere. But the Pygmy ministers of Chicago in their vapid, and to some extent blasphemous, utterances last Sunday morning on the San Francisco cataclysm attempted to dethrone God in His Own universe. . . . One fellow argued from the Book of Job that God does not punish sin by temporal afflictions. . . . But we remember that only a few years ago on Good Friday night of all the nights of the year many of the wealthy citizens of San Francisco assembled together with lewd women in one of the most luxurious mansions of the city and carried their hellish orgies so far that they kicked the globes off the chandeliers, we shall be inclined at least to abstain from asserting that subterranean gases, 'faults', and other seismic agencies were the principal and only cause of nature's convulsions."

There are people still living, perhaps, who believe that the earthquake was an act of Divine Justice —punishment for a "wicked" city. But then, there were also those who thought that the quake had been caused, in part at least, by man's continued "dabbling in electricity." Another wrote a long tract to explain that "airquakes" which followed the earth tremor were the real source of damage.

In the first weeks following the fire, the wife of Ex-governor James Budd predicted that there would be another big quake and announced at the same time that she had foretold the first one. San Francisco's *Mining and Scientific Press,* which carried the motto "Science has no enemy save the ignorant" on its masthead, had this to say about Mrs. Budd's prophetic talents:

". . . It appears that despite her belief in an impending cataclysm, the lady in question bought a $1500 piano two days before April 18. We are informed that the lady possesses a private observatory, for she uses a strong glass whereby she keeps tabs on the peculiar antics of several stars that have stayed up late and otherwise misbehaved. As to the 'strong glass'—that is a fruitful stimulant to sooth-saying; but we want to know whether it was Scotch or Bourbon."

Knowledge of the basic causes of earthquakes in

Fault trace passed directly under barn on Skinner ranch near Olema. Vertical displacement was noticeable here. (Branner Library)

Abutment of the bridge near Chittenden, on the Pajaro River fractured by force of the fault thrust. (Branner Library)

Sidewalks along Capp Street in the City lurched and tilted as the unfirm ground beneath it settled. Railway tracks, background, were laid directly on street surface, carried debris-removal cars. (Bear Photo Service)

general, and the San Francisco quake specifically, has not been materially expanded in the years since 1906. The California State Division of Mines made a simple summary of the extent of man's understanding following the San Francisco earthquake of March 22, 1957. That quake has been called by one 1906 survivor "nothing but an aftershock of the big one." The Division's *Mineral Service Information* said this:

"Nearly all destructive earthquakes have been the result of sudden movements of blocks of the earth's crust along breaks called 'faults.' Rock, which makes up the material of the earth, is elastic and may yield to stresses by slow creep over long periods of time. When the elastic limit of the rock is exceeded at any point, or friction along an old fault surface is overcome, an abrupt movement may take place causing an earthquake. The underlying reasons for accumulations of stresses in rocks of the outer part of the earth are little understood; however, such stresses and rock displacements are most frequent along the unstable margins of continental platforms and the ocean deeps. One such belt on the earth that is particularly active is the margin of the Pacific ocean. . . . California and Nevada, located in this seismically active Pacific belt, have had approximately 95 percent of the perceptible earthquakes in the United States."

In 1906, the land masses slipped on either side of an old break—the now-famous San Andreas Fault.

The subterranean displacement was deep. No one observed the actual rocks that slipped one against the other, but after the 1906 quake you could have seen the ragged line that ran 200 miles along the San Andreas Fault. This surface rupture was, like the fallen

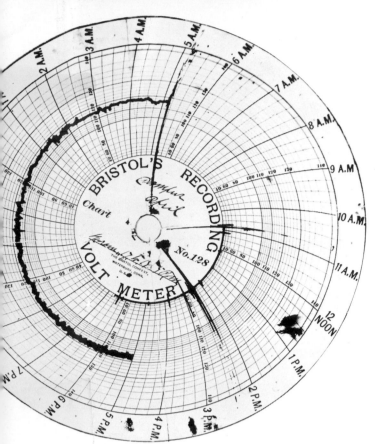

Stanford's recording voltmeter worked as a seismograph the morning of the quake. When the quake hit, the pen inking the slowly revolving disc flailed about wildly and marked the moment of the shock. (Stanford Collection)

The fault long ago formed Crystal Springs Lakes in San Mateo County. In 1906, the rift offset the road now called Skyline Boulevard where it crosses the lakes on an earth-fill dam. Road is extensively used today.

buildings, merely an outward manifestation of the underlying trouble. The surface furrow resulted from, rather than caused, the earthquake. This furrow, which indicated a maximum earth shift of twenty-one feet between points on the fault, is the longest such rift to appear in recorded history.

The earth displacement, as the map shows, ran from Point Arena on the north coast to San Juan Bautista, site of one of California's early missions, near Salinas in the south. The line is almost straight and, although it passes through such natural depressions as the Crystal Springs Lakes and Tomales Bay, the fault climbs into the mountains behind Palo Alto and continues for dozens of miles before again hitting a "natural" path.

Stories were told of the earth opening up and swallowing cattle at the time of the quake. The fact is that up in Marin county, near Olema, *one* frightened cow ran into a muddy, badly disrupted section of the crack and became so badly mired that nothing was left to do but bury her on the spot.

Northward, in a quicksilver mine near Guerneville on the Russian River, three men were killed when a tunnel collapsed. This was overlooked by the rumor makers, and is one of the forgotten stories of the earthquake.

Other than at this mine, most of man's underground burrowing was unharmed. Some artesian wells were wrecked in Santa Clara, but this was the extent of serious damage to mines and wells in the fault region.

Once the dust had settled, geologists and historians began to poke through the record books. Earthquakes had been recorded in California back in the eighteenth century. In 1769, seven years before the founding of Mission Dolores, Portola wrote of a quake at the Santa Ana River, which his party named Rio de Jesus de los Temblores. In 1808, eighteen damaging shakes were felt in San Francisco between June 21 and July 17. Four years later, a killer quake struck southern California, causing damage over many hundreds of miles. Thirty to forty-five Indians were killed at Mission San Juan Capistrano when an eighty-foot tower fell in on them during mass. Mission Santa Inez, 170 miles away, was completely destroyed.

One of California's worst quakes occurred in 1872. Sparsely settled Inyo County was racked severely, and most of Southern California and the Sierra Nevada region were badly shaken. The quake was felt as far away as Kentucky and Mexico City. At Lone Pine, a mere dozen miles from Mount Whitney, fifty-two of fifty-nine buildings were totally wrecked, and sixty

In San Francisco, Valencia Street pavement flexed and bulged where filled land slumped six feet near Eighteenth. (Bancroft Library)

Heavy steel tracks bent and buckled in San Francisco streets when the undulating, incredibly powerful waves swept across the rock and sand and carelessly gathered fill that made up the surface of the City. New Post Office is on the left, above. (Bancroft Library)

A young lady, dressed in the height of fashion, drapes her bustle over the edge of a fissure formed during the quake near Milpitas. The area was miles from the fault, but considerable change in the terrain was found.
(Branner Library)

In San Mateo County an officer sits on a valve box at the point where rift crossed Pilarcitos pipeline. Earth movement was so violent in this locale that pieces of the sod were overturned and thrown two or three feet. (Branner Library)

people were killed or injured. In Yosemite Valley, to quote the San Francisco *Bulletin* ". . . many rocks fell, filling the valley with smoke and dust. The largest trees waved to and fro and were bent about like mere twigs."

The Far Western states have no monopoly on earthquakes, however. The distinction of the "biggest" belongs to the Middle West, where in 1808 the granddaddy of all shook the Mississippi basin for fifty-four days. The earth's surface in some sections dropped thirty to forty feet. Thomas Jefferson had purchased the continent's heart from the French five years before, but the land still belonged to the Indians. The story of this great quake failed to enter the American tradition.

The Charleston earthquake of 1886, however, was well remembered, until 1906, as the nation's worst. Ninety-six were killed in the old South Carolina town, and most of the buildings were left uninhabitable.

No American earthquake, before or since, has been studied and written about as much as the California shake of 1906.

The Carnegie Institution of Washington published an exhaustive treatise prepared by a commission appointed by Governor Pardee and headed by Prof. Andrew C. Lawson of the University of California. The two volume work they prepared set a world standard in earthquake reporting.

As bad as some of her earthquakes have been, the United States has had it relatively easy. One of the worst in North America occurred in 1773 in Guatemala City, which was then a growing center of trade and third largest Latin American City. The catastrophic earthquake wiped out most of the town of 60,000. The city was never rebuilt. The survivors abandoned the ruins and moved inland twenty miles to build the city we know today.

But the worst in the Western hemisphere do not begin to measure up to some of the appalling shakes of Europe and Asia.

At least thirty earthquakes have claimed more than 20,000 lives; ten have taken more than 60,000, and five of these took more than 100,000 lives. The largest toll in history was recorded in 1556, in Shensi, China, when 830,000 lives were lost.

In this century, two quakes have taken more than 100,000. Ten cities and 180,000 lives were destroyed by the 1920 earthquake in Kansu Province, China, while the better-known Tokyo quake of 1923 killed 143,000.

The Lisbon earthquake of 1755 is considered to have been the most terrifying of all time. Early on the morning of November first a six-second tremor threw

Eight miles to the northeast of Boulder Creek, this land-slide buried a sawmill and six men beneath 125 feet of debris.

Alluvial lands on the Pajaro River near Watsonville dropped 7 feet. Tree, right, belongs in orchard, above.

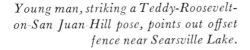

Young man, striking a Teddy-Roosevelt-on-San Juan-Hill pose, points out offset fence near Searsville Lake.

Almost a mile of track slid into the drink on the coast below the City. A highway now runs along the cliff. (Photos Courtesy of Branner Library)

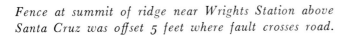

Fence at summit of ridge near Wrights Station above Santa Cruz was offset 5 feet where fault crosses road.

down almost every building in the town. The quake was followed by a tidal wave which arrived in the harbor at the same time a huge fissure opened to swallow a newly-built marble dock crowded with thousands of panic-stricken Portuguese. Somewhere between 50,000 and 60,000 were killed. Later measurements showed that 600 feet of water stood in the spot where the quay had been.

Sand craterlets formed in the Watsonville area as a result of severe dislocations in the rocks below the surface. Spontaneous springs poured from new openings in the earth following the quake, and sand carried to the surface by the flowing water was deposited. (Branner Library)

Four months after the San Francisco earthquake and fire, Valparaiso, Chile, was visited by earthquake. Perhaps 2000 were killed, and hundreds of millions of dollars in damage done by the tremor and by the fires which followed. There was no connection between the two, other than coincidence in time and magnitude. The fact is that the western continental shelves of both North and South America are earthquake country, and until some distant time, hundreds and thousands of gener- ations into history, they will remain earthquake coun- try.

For what it's worth, one historical analysis showed that an earthquake the power of the 1906 quake will occur once every 200 years in the same region. David Starr Jordan, President of Stanford, noted that forty years seemed to be a natural interval and therefore, half seriously, predicted the next first-class shake would come in 1946. He was off eleven years: March 22, 1957, was the date. Of course, there had been a re- spectable number of plaster-cracking, dish-rattling quakes in the interim, but the little ones don't count.

When will the next one hit? No one knows. Perry Byerly, the noted University of California seismologist, put it this way: "The further you are from the last big earthquake, the nearer you are to the next."

154

Only part of the 600-mile stretch of the San Andreas Fault shuddered the morning of April 18, 1906, and it was but one in an eon-long series. The western continental shelf is earthquake country and will remain so beyond man's farthest vision into the future. ABOVE, San Francisco lies to the right of the main fault break which passes under the ocean from Mussel Rock, lower left, and re-enters at the depression near Bolinas in Marin County, top left. Looking to the south of San Francisco, BELOW, the fault enters at Mussel Rock, just out of sight, and traverses San Mateo and Santa Clara counties and beyond. Crystal Springs Lakes, long narrow bodies near center of the photo lie directly on the rift. Half Moon Bay curls around on the right, and Monterey Bay lies shrouded in the dim distance. Suburb towns, San Bruno, Millbrae, Burlingame crowd the Peninsula on the left. Mushrooming tracts expand up the hills of Pacifica, right, including one which sits right on the fault. The 1957 quake caused some damage in Westlake (out of view at bottom of picture), a development built by the omnivorous granddaddy of Bay Area tract builders, Henry Doelger. That shake was given a 5.5 rating on the Richter scale—puny beside the 8.25 score of the 1906 wallop. (Official Photographs, U. S. Navy)

155

FROM

THE

ASHES

Workman pauses with his back to a tiny part of the debris which chokes the City's streets and cellars. View is down Montgomery toward Telegraph Hill beyond Mills Building. (Bear Photo Service)

At the time of the fire, James D. Phelan had already served as Mayor of the City and was later to become Senator from California. He suffered a great loss when his uninsured office building at O'Farrell and Market burned, but he joined his political enemy, Mayor Schmitz, to lead San Francisco through the critical period. His contribution to the welfare of the City appears, in retrospect, greater than Funston's or Schmitz's. (Society of California Pioneers)

"**N**O ONE whose opinion is worth a rap entertains a doubt as to San Francisco's future," said Tirey L. Ford, Solicitor General of the United Railways, and he was right. Not a businessman left the City, and the first contracts to rebuild in the downtown district were written while the ashes were still hot.

Will Irwin wrote a beautiful eulogy for San Francisco in the New York *Sun* called "The City That Was." It began:

"The old San Francisco is dead. The gayest, lightest hearted, most pleasure-loving city of this continent, and in many ways the most interesting and romantic, is a horde of huddled refugees living among ruins."

But the "City That Was" was gone, and the men who were ready to rebuild her did not look back. James D. Phelan, whose financial loss was more than $1 million and whose grief at the passing of the City must certainly have been as great as any man's, dismissed the past with this seeming irreverence:

"San Francisco was no ancient city. It was the recent creation of the Pioneers and possessed the accumulated stores of only a couple of generations. Its temples, monuments and public buildings were not of conspicuous merit or of great value. There was, in fine, nothing destroyed that cannot be speedily rebuilt."

$600,000 in gold is loaded onto a dray parked beside the Mint—first money to leave vaults after the fire. (California Historical Society)

One of the first business signs went up on the wrecked building, left, at the corner of California and Kearny. (California Historical Society)

And that is precisely what Phelan and the rest of San Francisco set out to do.

One of the first problems faced was that of getting money into circulation. All the banks had burned to the ground, and many people, including some of the wealthiest, found themselves without a nickel. The only available money was stored in the vaults of the mint, and it was by an ingenious arrangement with mint officials that banks served their customers. All opened emergency offices as soon as the fire ended. Many opened for business in the home of one of the directors or the bank president. They were without records, but every depositor who wanted money and was recognized by the bank officers was given a counter-signed draft that the mint officials honored in gold coin. At that time, Californians had about as much use for paper money as they did for copper pennies. The gold standard had been a grass-roots standard for more than fifty years.

The E. S. Heller home served as temporary office of several concerns for weeks following the fire. The house, still in use as a residence at 2020 Jackson, remains virtually unchanged. Genthe took this a few days after fire. (California Palace of the Legion)

Safe experts set up boxes in front of their former office and wait for the trade. Learning a good lesson from the Chicago and Baltimore fires, San Franciscans waited several weeks while the steel and concrete cooled before trying to open their safes. As a result, no major loss was recorded due to a premature opening. (California Historical Society)

A ruined downtown building is dynamited. (Bancroft Library)

In quiet eloquence, these signs on Market Street tell the story of San Francisco's determination to carry on without looking back. Buckled columns and ruined walls are part of the past, and commerce won't wait to mourn. Gutted St. Francis Hotel in background. (Bear Photo Service)

Market Street business took on a lively carnival air before serious rebuilding began. (California Historical Society)

Many out-of-town banks refused to honor checks drawn on San Francisco banks, fearing a panic when the vaults were opened. The panic never materialized. San Francisco had always been a creditor city, with large deposits in Eastern banks.

Within six weeks, every banking house in the City was doing business as it had before. A good many of them had built temporary structures right over their old vaults. It took only until the week of June 23, 1906, before bank clearings eclipsed the amount for the corresponding week in 1905, $30,999,862 to $30,545,176. San Francisco was proud to point out that the figure topped the combined clearings of Los Angeles, Denver, Seattle, and Salt Lake City for the week.

A "Committee of Forty on the Reconstruction of San Francisco" was formed in the days following the fire, and subcommittees on every possible project threw themselves to the problem of rebuilding. Special groups were set up on assessments, sewers, hospitals, widening the streets, parks, reservoirs, boulevards, revenue and taxation, condemnation of old buildings, the Burnham Plan, and more.

Announcements of plans to rebuild came thick and fast. On April 23 plans to rebuild both the Mills Building and Raphael Weill's White House were revealed. Weill, a *bon vivant* of the old school said this:

"The White House will be rebuilt, and it will be better than ever. I have enough left to buy an annuity

Nothing would hold once the first shock passed and the realization it was time to go to work had arrived. Upper floors of the Merchant's Exchange, left, were still a shambles after the lower floor was hastily refurbished. California Street is choked with traffic—not idle observers, but people with a job to do. (California Historical Society)

Mayor Eugene Schmitz enjoyed a brief journey into glory following the fire. His height, bearing, and dashing black beard make him easy to spot, center right. Boss Abe Ruef stands at his left elbow as a group of City and United Railway officials pose before a special car in front of the Ferry Building. Patrick Calhoun, head of United Railways and later under severe attack for bribery is fifth to the right of the Mayor. Below, Schmitz stands on the steps of the first trolley on Market. Ruef waves from the window. (Edward Zelinsky; Thomas C. Boyle)

and live like a fighting cock for the rest of my days; but none of that for me. I am going into the work of rebuilding with all my soul. I am 70 years old, but I love San Francisco with a love that is filial, and I'm going to work at the restoration of the city as if I were only 30."

Plans for the first brand-new building in downtown San Francisco were made public on the same day, Monday the twenty-third. Design of the eighteen-story Humboldt Bank Building, which was to be located a block west of the Call Building on Market, was rushed, and the builder announced hopefully that the new "skyscraper" would be finished by July of 1907.

Fillmore Street, seven blocks west of Van Ness Avenue, was a growing shopping district before the fire, but the real-estate boom along this street after the fire was something to behold. Every house and store was snapped up on leases at rates unheard of a week before, and then many of the new leases were sublet at twice the price a few weeks later.

Monday after the fire, 300 plumbers were at work on the sewers and water pipes alone. Two weeks were allotted to get the system into working order and service all the houses left habitable behind the fire.

James B. Stetson, whose house on Van Ness was spared largely by his own efforts, later wrote:

"We had water in the house on the 1st of May, glass in the windows on the 16th of May, gas on the 5th of June, electric lights on the 7th of June, and cooked on the streets until the 8th of May."

The Stetsons were fortunate in having their chimney inspected as soon as they did. Many were still cooking out of doors months later.

Several kinds of business sprang up in the first weeks among the ruins. Souvenir peddlers and minor restaurateurs set up ramshackle quarters all along Market Street and in the commercial district to the north. Blacksmiths had business waiting for them before they could set up makeshift forges, and the safe experts had a field day. Nine days after the fire, the safe crackers were ready to help hundreds of businessmen salvage what they could. The Chicago and Baltimore fires, of 1871 and 1904, taught San Francisco patience. In both of the earlier conflagrations, safe owners had been in a hurry to see if money and papers had come through unharmed. Often the rush of fresh air into the box, as it was opened, burned everything within to a crisp. Not

Overloaded auto and streetcar make way past the Emporium on Market. A new store was built around this façade. (Bear Photo Company)

162

Demolition of the shattered Hearst Building at Third and Market was well covered, photographically. Upper left view looking down Kearny, and the one above, up Third. (California Historical Society; Bancroft Library)

Workmen tighten block and tackle to pull scrap from First National Bank ruins before building is demolished.
(Bear Photo Service)

A spellbound crowd watches as one of the ruined towers of St. Dominic's Church is blasted by wrecking crew.
(Bear Photo Service)

Market Street at intersection of Geary, Kearny, in August, 1906. Photo taken from Monadnock Building. (*Morton-Waters Company*)

"LARGE RIB STEAK—25¢ *With Tea, Coffee, or Milk*," the specialty of the house, shared billing with Dr. Kilmer's Swamp Root Kidney, Liver, and Bladder Remedy. Food was cheap and simple in the many sidewalk restaurants, but the fare a great improvement over the relief kitchens. (*California Historical Society*)

164

a safe in San Francisco, at least not an important one, was cracked before two weeks were up. As a result, the contents of San Francisco's safes came through toasted at worst, and unharmed in many cases.

Van Ness was even busier after the first few weeks had passed. Most of the buildings were residences, but the character of this boulevard was to be forever changed. The mansions which had been saved on the west side were converted into department stores and restaurants and haberdasheries, and as on Fillmore, any habitable place became worth twice its weight in gold. Bullock and Jones settled in an old house at the corner of Van Ness and Eddy, while the White House held forth further up at the corner of Pine. The "new" Emporium sat between the two at Van Ness and Post. It wasn't long before the only building left unchanged on the street was huge, ungainly St. Mary's Cathedral at the corner of O'Farrell, where it still sits.

Along the east side of the street, temporary stores with wide display windows were hastily built. What seemed like hundreds of flags flew above the buildings on both sides, giving the street a festive air during the four years it remained the city's retail center. A store owner not only flew an American flag and another with the name of his firm, but often the flag of the country of his birth. The circus air which prevailed through these years may not have made sense to some dour souls, but it was fun for almost everyone.

San Francisco's newspapers were well established before the first week following the fire had ended. The *Chronicle, Call* and *News* all published from the office of the Oakland *Herald* during the interim. The *Examiner* used the presses of the Oakland *Tribune* until new machinery arrived from Los Angeles. The *Examiner*, which had to rebuild San Francisco headquarters from scratch, set up the presses and published from Oakland until the new Hearst Building was com-

When the time came to open the safes, they were attacked with a vengeance by workmen as owners stood by. (Bancroft Library)

The blackened marble walls of the Fairmont Hotel were left sound when the fire passed, but all of the newly completed interior had to be redone. The men are standing at the corner of Mason and California streets. (Edward Zelinsky)

A.P. HOTALING & Co

Looking down Montgomery St. from Broadway, Saturday morning, April 21, 1906. Arrow points to our Stores and Warehouses

The warehouse of A. P. Hotaling Co. lay within the boundaries of the only downtown island of unburned buildings. Their business was whisky distribution, and they lost little time in letting the world know they were still in business. This card, showing Montgomery Street leading to Market in the distance, carried a piece of doggerel on the other side that everyone learned. The verse, written by Charles K. Field in answer to the fanatics who claimed God caused the City's destruction because it was such a sinful place, went like this:

"If as some say, God spanked the town
For being over frisky,
Why did he burn the Churches down
And save Hotaling's Whisky?"
(California Historical Society)

It didn't take much to set up souvenir shops along Market, the main thoroughfare for tourists from Oakland and points east. Shoppers examine china, silver at lower Market Street stand, LEFT, *and haggle at the corner of Powell,* BELOW. *Gourd-shaped Chinese liquor bottles, like those on nearest box, haven't changed to this day. (Bear Photo Service)*

pleted. But the *Call* was back in semirefurbished quarters in the Spreckels Building less than six weeks after the quake, and the *Chronicle* was back on Newspaper Row by the middle of July.

The rental situation was bad all over town. By November all rents shot up to the point where anything, anywhere was worth twice what it had commanded in spring. A story in the November 1906 *Overland Monthly* told of the trying situation:

"Today there is not a single dwelling to be had. They are in such demand that whenever a new building is started, all the flats are rented before the foundation is laid . . . prospective tenants who hear of a building being let, trace up the contractor, interview the owner, and pay a deposit on the flat before the building operations are commenced."

166

Brand spanking new in the middle of a wasteland, the Regal Shoe Store signs fairly shout at the passing traffic. But the small, crudely lettered sign on the sidewalk carries the message that all San Francisco wanted to read: "OPEN . . . Doing Business at the Old Stand" (Bear Photo Service)

Dunham, Carrigan & Hayden, a hardware firm founded the year gold was discovered in the Sierras, was bequeathed a mountain of marvelous rubble by the fire. The useless remains of picks, house jacks, animal traps, pipe, valves, locks, files, conduit, drills, bits, chain, grinders, and springs mark the end of an era and the beginning of another. (California Historical Society)

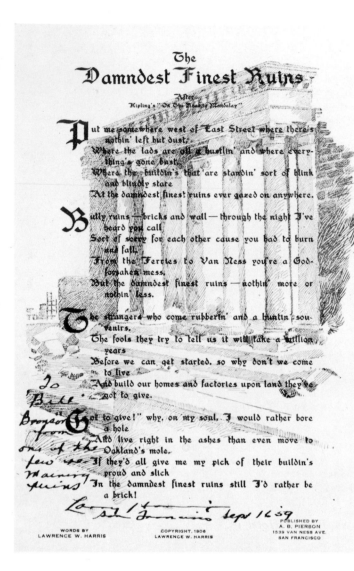

The
Damndest Finest Ruins

After
Kipling's "On The Road to Mandalay"

Put me somewhere west of East Street where there's
nothin' left but dust;
Where the lads are all a hustlin' and where everything's gone bust,
Where the buildin's that are standin' sort of blink
and blindly stare
At the damndest finest ruins ever gazed on anywhere.

Bully ruins—bricks and wall—through the night I've
heard you call
Sort of sorry for each other cause you had to burn
and fall.
From the Ferries to Van Ness you're a Godforsaken mess,
But the damndest finest ruins—nothin' more or
nothin' less.

The strangers who come rubberin' and a huntin' souvenirs,
The fools they try to tell us it will take a million
years
Before we can get started, so why don't we come
to live
And build our homes and factories upon land they've
got to give.

"Got to give!" why, on my soul, I would rather bore
a hole
And live right in the ashes than even move to
Oakland's mole.
If they'd all give me my pick of their buildin's
proud and slick
In the damndest finest ruins still I'd rather be
a brick!

To Bill Bronson from one of the few Maenng ruins San Francisco Sept 16 59

WORDS BY
LAWRENCE W. HARRIS

COPYRIGHT, 1906
LAWRENCE W. HARRIS

PUBLISHED BY
A. B. PIERSON
1539 VAN NESS AVE.
SAN FRANCISCO

Larry Harris's splendid verses, still ringing with the brash, confident spirit of the post-fire period, will live as long as the City itself. The inscription shows that his wit, like his poem, has not suffered with the years.

The cleanup job was, like the fire, the biggest man ever faced. An estimated 6½ billion bricks fell during the earthquake and fire, and the job of clearing away debris was judged greater than that of digging the Panama Canal.

The first thing to be done was to dynamite dangerous shells which had resisted complete destruction by fire. On April 23, the Odd Fellows Hall at Seventh and Market half a block from the main Post Office was blown apart by 750 pounds of explosive. The charge not only destroyed the remains of the lodge hall, but "damn near" ruined the Post Office. To quote the *San Francisco News:*

". . . all windows, transoms and skylights were shattered. Doors were torn from the hinges, marble cornices dislodged and heavy lawbooks from the U. S. Attorney's office were blown clear out of the building."

City Hall's majestic dome stood untouched as rebuilding gathered momentum. It wasn't until 1912 that the City overwhelmingly approved a bond issue for a new Civic Center, and by that time the rest of the town had been transformed. Many features of the Burnham Plan were incorporated in the center, but the latest addition, Brooks' Mole Hall, was the fruit of later planning.

"If you can't give it away, sell it." Why anyone surrounded by thousands of acres of junk would be interested in paying for a tiny bit of it may seem something of a mystery. Actually, some of the twisted, fused, and melted mementos which have come down to this day are museum pieces—in San Francisco. (California Historical Society)

RIGHT: Water and sewer repairs were first on the list of City projects. Fortunately, blueprint copies of City's power, gas, and sewer systems were on file at U.C. library. (Bancroft Library)

The towers of Temple Emanu El rise above the temporary St. Francis Hotel in Union Square. Nob Hill, LEFT. (California Historical Society)

Genthe's poignant glimpse of a lonely Chinese stoically trudging through the wreckage of Chinatown is sharpened in contrast to the scene below taken six years after the fire. Fairmont Hotel in distance, above, and corner of California and Dupont, below. (California Historical Society)

Horseshoers and sign painters joined the sidewalk restaurateurs and safecrackers as the first to renew commerce in the stricken town. (Society of California Pioneers)

The blast added $100,000 damage to the Post Office.

Some buildings were so stoutly built that they had to be taken apart bit by bit. The Palace Hotel was almost indestructible: it cost $90,000 to haul her thirty million bricks down.

The City's debris was largely carted away in railroad cars. Much of the first rubble was dumped in that elbow of San Francisco Bay called Mission Bay. When Mission Bay had been filled to the limit, two-thousand-ton barges were used to tow the crumbled brick and ashes out to the neighborhood of Mile Rock—the lighthouse west of the Golden Gate not exactly a mile from anything—and there a good part of the "City That Was" still lies.

Railroad tracks were laid all through the downtown sections to hasten the removal. "Donkey" steam engines were used to haul countless tons of debris from the basements, and thousands of horses were worked to death in the first year and a half. The SPCA wagon worked three shifts a day to cart off the dead animals. Rufus Steele wrote in 1909 that on ". . . lower Market Street somewhere, an equine statue should be erected to the memory of the fifteen thousand four-legged heroes whose

170

March 3, 1907, was official house-cleaning day, and thousands of merchants, students, artisans, clubwomen, and other sundry slices of San Francisco life turned to. ABOVE, *a small crowd collects to watch young volunteers line up for instructions. The pictures to the* RIGHT *show the streets being scraped and swept free of the fine debris left behind when the main job of clearing the town was done.* (California Historical Society; Bancroft Library)

exhausted carcasses were carted off to the bone yard . . ."

To those of a later generation, San Francisco's response to the total destruction of Chinatown seems strangely out of place. No tears were spilled for the passing of this quaint and world-famous quarter. Instead, the loss of Chinatown was hailed as one of the blessings of the fire. Pierre Beringer in the *Overland Monthly* said:

"Fire has reclaimed to civilization and cleanliness the Chinese ghetto, and no Chinatown will be permitted in the borders of the city. Some other provision will be made for the caring of the orientals."

"The new Chinatown will be at Hunter's Point," added the *Independent,* unequivocably.

This notion was repeated by many responsible people, all of whom forgot that San Francisco's Chinese were well qualified to take care of themselves and had no desire in the world to move elsewhere. Chinatown was rebuilt right where it fell, and there wasn't any hesitation about it.

As a matter of fact, the architecture of many new buildings was authentic Chinese, where the original buildings had been put up by Yankees in the early years.

Men from the Union Iron Works stream for trolleys at the end of a working day in May, 1906. Since the yard's equipment had not been damaged, orders piled sky high. This shot was taken looking down Twentieth Street from Kentucky. (Society of California Pioneers)

In less than a week, Fillmore Street became the City's main business section and traffic jammed its length. Although Van Ness eventually assumed the role of main "temporary" business thoroughfare, Fillmore boomed like never before or since. (Oakland Tribune)

Two new steel and concrete office buildings rise on a bustling, broken stage at California Street where it meets Market, front, and Drumm, center. The tall flagpole, right, which survived the fire, had replaced an offensive fountain given by Henry Coggswell, San Francisco temperance leader. Fountain torn down years before by a band of indignant students from the University of California. (Morton-Waters Company)

Many 1906 landmarks are visible in this shot taken west of Fifth on Mission. Ferry Building, right, St. Francis, left. Mint stands like a fortress in the front center. Flags wave over the shells of two towers in construction: the Whittell and Humboldt Bank buildings. (Morton-Waters Company)

Crumpled girders and columns made the Mutual Life Insurance Building unsafe, but it was too big to blow apart. Dismantlers, BELOW, stand on building's top floor. (Bancroft Library)

Long strings of gondolas moved across City streets on special tracks to carry debris away. This picture, taken in June of 1906, shows workmen dumping rubble in South of Market train. (Society of California Pioneers)

Before the fire, professional Chinatown guides escorted visitors to the city through the quarter. Chinatown of old had a wicked reputation—it was said that tunnels laced the ground beneath the streets to a depth of eighty feet, and that far from the sight of any Occidental, slave girls were bought and sold. Visitors were taken to "opium dens" where old addicts would perform. It is true that many Chinese smoked opium in those days, but to most it played the same role in social life that alcohol did for the non-Oriental.

Before the days of bulldozers, shovels and wheelbarrows did the job. Rear of Monadnock Building, left. (Society of California Pioneers)

NEW PLAN OF CITY ADOPTED BY THE CITIZENS' COMMITTEE

The above map shows the plan for widened streets adopted by the Citizens' Committee and provisionally approved by the Supervisors. The heavy black lines show the widened streets, as well as the new diagonal streets which have not yet been named, and the winding streets by means of which easy access may be secured to Nob Hill.

| YOUNG WOMAN IS | FEARS HUSBAND | MOVES BOOKS TO |
| BRANDED A THIEF | WILL KILL HER | PLACE OF SAFETY |

The Burnham Plan was adopted a month after the fire, but none of the bold new streets were ever cut through.

Tait's, burned out of the Flood Building, took over the Wallace residence on Van Ness Avenue and became one of the most popular restaurants of the reconstruction period. (Bear Photo Service)

Army Engineers announced on the last day of the fire that the Ferry Building should be razed, but they were ignored. Restoration was well underway in summer of 1906. (Bear Photo Service)

Banners snapped and rustled in the afternoon breeze above Van Ness Avenue for several years following the fire. Spreckels mansion, beyond White House flag, was eventually demolished. Note the casual traffic pattern. (Morton-Waters Company)

In 1906, not all were sure what was going to happen, and after the ashes cooled, some of the writers began to talk with a little more sense. One observer in the May 1906 issue of *Overland Monthly* noted this:

"It may lack the familiar holes, corners and smells of Chinatown, but it will be more agreeable to the eye if not quite so piquant to the nose. And even of this we cannot be too sure, for it is said that the Chinese will insist on rebuilding on the old site. Possibly the new San Francisco will not be so joyous a place to the unregenerate nor so painful a spot to the pious as formerly, but even of this it is not well to be too positive."

Today, opium and slave girls are gone, and gambling has retreated behind locked doors, but Chinatown still runs its own business with a minimum of interference from City Hall. The big change lies in San Francisco's attitude. If anyone suggested tearing Chinatown down and asking the Chinese to move elsewhere, the idea would find about as much support as a plan to dismantle the Golden Gate Bridge.

Darkness brought the Barbary Coast to life. Although rejuvenated by the fire, the section slowly degenerated and is like a ghost town today. (California Historical Society)

Pacific Street's Barbary Coast, foreground, was one pocket of the City almost completely forgotten in the commotion. Cliffs of Telegraph Hill fill the background. (California Historical Society)

THE WASP

Another Earthquake in San Francisco
(From the New York World)

The world was shocked not six months after the fire when the City ruled that Japanese would have to go to separate schools. The drive against the Japanese, whose capacity for work and respect for the law are legendary, was prompted by the fact that several Japanese-born males in their middle and late teens attended public grammar schools. Teddy Roosevelt stuck his unwelcome nose into the matter and quashed it summarily. The rebuke smarted but the issue was closed.

Spreckel's Call Building was speedily restored. The lower floors were opened a month after the fire on an emergency basis, while the upper floors were refinished. Once San Francisco's tallest skyscraper, it is overshadowed today by a score of others. And you won't recognize it unless you know where to look. The whole exterior was covered with square slabs of white marble after World War II, and name was changed to Central Tower. (Society of California Pioneers)

It is pleasant to think the fire wiped out not Chinatown, but the blot of unreasoning prejudice against the Chinese which for so long remained California's shame. The devotion of Chinese workers to their employers after the fire helped change the public's mind, as did the swift way they found work and left relief roles. No other identifiable group, save perhaps the Japanese, was so quick to look for and find work that permitted them to leave the camps.

It was not all sweetness and smiles after rebuilding commenced, however. The workingman was often a

Bubonic plague broke out in the City in May of 1907, and 77 of the 160 victims died in the epidemic. It was the second eruption of Black Death in seven years, and this time the health authorities clamped down hard. Six and a half million square feet of concrete flooring were poured in potential rat breeding areas, and two million rats were killed with poisoned bait.

CITIZENS' HEALTH COMMITTEE
Headquarters Room 1233 Merchants' Exchange

The Plague in San Francisco and

Its Extermination

The dreaded "Bubonic Plague" has reappeared in San Francisco since the fire and is gaining ground.

Should the Plague continue to show a marked increase, San Francisco will probably be quarantined. This would be a death blow to the industrial life of the city and would bring ruin to our people and our homes.

The Federal, State and City health authorities are fighting this disease for our benefit. To insure success, your co-operation is imperative.

This Plague is primarily a disease of the Rat.

The infection is transmitted by the Flea.

The Flea living on the infected Rat becomes infected.

If the infected Flea bites a human being, that person becomes infected with the Plague.

The percentage of infected Rats has increased three-fold since September, 1907.

The Flea disappears in San Francisco during the winter and reappears with dry and warm weather. The coming of the Flea cannot be prevented, but we can combat the Rat, the source and the breeder of the Plague.

It is incumbent upon all to wage a relentless war on the Rat.

YOUR DUTY

Trap and Poison Rats !

Obey the Sanitary Laws of the City !

Have your Premises Inspected !

177

Millions of feet of redwood and fir were carried to San Francisco from the north by a fleet of rugged lumber schooners. (*Society of California Pioneers*)

Francis Heney and Rudolph Spreckels were controversial leaders of the graft prosecutions. Heney was made Assistant District Attorney through the efforts of Spreckels and for several years the two were at the center of a storm —judged either the City's finest citizens or vicious, self-seeking persecutors, depending on the point of view.

Santa Claus Remembers Them

Appropriate gifts for Gene, Jerry and Abe, the Three Disgraces of our Municipal Administration

target in the "capitalistic" press. The Christmas issue of *The Wasp,* a San Francisco weekly, took this swipe:

"One of the most remarkable of the achievements of the period of reconstruction has been work done in restoring the street railroad system of the city. Of a total of 250 miles of rail before the fire, 220 were in operation and all would be in a few weeks.

"Thousands of laborers have been kept working night and day on the tracks and it has been very difficult to find enough hands. The men employed are mostly Greeks and Turks. A worse lot of loafers was never seen. They get high wages though they would be dear at $1 a day."

The fact that they were the same "loafers" who actually did the work referred to as a "remarkable achievement" seems to have slipped the mind of the writer.

It had been in July that the debris cleaners had organized to demand $2.50 per eight-hour day in place of the $1.72 to $2.00 they were taking home from a nine-hour stint. At the same time carpenters were making $4 to $5, bricklayers $6 to $8, and plumbers $6 to $7 a day.

E. P. Erwin, in his tirade against the unions (*Overland Monthly,* "The Matter with San Francisco"), had this to say about a "typical" union leader:

". . . foreign born, un-American boss who holds sway over the waterfront . . . Czar who rules over a few uncouth Greeks and Italians . . . a self-seeking demagogue who cares not for San Francisco, but merely for himself . . ."

This delicate appraisal was followed, however, by a bit of fairness:

"Not all the blame must be laid at the door of the unions. They are only part of the load the struggling City bears on her back. The workman gets only that which the richer and more powerful hold-up man leaves. And between welching insurance companies and extortionate demands of the lumber men and purveyors of other materials necessary for the City's rehabilitation, there is not always very much for the smaller robbers to take."

A strike of the carmen against the United Railways in 1907 drove deep to the core of the bad feeling between workingman and capitalist. During the strike, union members were fined if found using the management and scab-driven streetcars. Special wagons and other makeshift conveyances were pressed into service by the unions for their members and sympathizers.

There was bickering, bitterness, recrimination, all right, but somehow San Francisco got the job done. And the job was not only done, but it was done faster and better than anyone thought possible. In three years

Teddy Roosevelt's Great White Fleet steamed through the Golden Gate in Spring of 1908 to salute the City. Telegraph Hill, foreground, is choked with spectators. (California Historical Society)

West on Geary from Market in February of 1908. Compare this view with one taken 1½ years earlier on page 164. (California Historical Society)

almost all of the burned area was rebuilt. All twenty-seven "fireproof" (class "A") buildings which went through the fire were restored, and seventy-seven more like them were added to the City's panorama. In 1909, more than half of America's steel and concrete buildings stood in San Francisco.

In three years the assessed valuation of the City was half again as much as it had been before the fire. Twenty thousand buildings—bigger, stronger, more modern than the 28,000 which went up in smoke—had been finished in that space of time.

And the Burnham Plan? Many thought that the fire had provided a clincher for a remodeled city. Benjamin Ide Wheeler spoke for many when he said, "For the first three weeks after the fire there was much reason to fear that the dual catastrophe might be crowned by a third disaster—the rebuilding of the City on the old plan."

Before the fire, the *Overland Monthly* praised the Burnham Plan warmly, and the article ended:

"Do not let it be simply—A dream, and a forgetting."

TODAY.

Transformation
of the
Business
Section
OF THE CITY
SINCE THE FIRE

1 YEAR LATER.

RUINS 1906.

The people of San Francisco were mighty proud of the way the town bounced back, and they weren't bashful about letting the world know about it. These views are from Nob Hill. (Bear Photo Service)

Year of the Exposition, 1915, is blazoned across top of the new Humboldt Bank Building in this view down Market Street taken in 1912. (California Historical Society)

But the City was in too much of a rush to think of "beautification," and it *was* forgotten.

With the exception of the Civic Center, no important change in the City's topography was made. It is true that Bayshore Highway was envisioned by Burnham, but this surely would have evolved by itself. The proposed alterations diminished in importance to those whose job it was to finance and build the new City when the potential delay and expense became obvious.

No story of the rebuilding of the City should omit one chapter which is not widely remembered today. The greed of grafters in City Hall grew in those hectic days. Property owners, contractors, and the utilities champed at the bit to get directly to the job of rebuilding. With plenty of ready cash, it was easy to pay under the counter for fast service on this permit or that inspection. The utilities, in particular, redoubled their efforts to gain advantage through bribery.

Abe Ruef's "paint eaters" and Mayor Schmitz himself couldn't stand the overwhelming prosperity, and they literally ran it into the ground. By Christmas of 1906, Ruef and Schmitz—the "Hero of the Hour" in April—were under indictment. Both were convicted of accepting bribes, and after much litigation, Abe Ruef went to prison.

It was a sticky affair, but good for the City. Pierre N. Beringer predicted this during the course of the scandal:

"San Francisco does things on a heroic scale always, and its political housecleaning will be as thorough as its physical cleaning by the fire."

The problem was handled directly. After the conviction, a temporary mayor was appointed from among the corrupt supervisors. Then a reform man, Dr. Edward R. Taylor, was elected to the board to fill the vacancy and was immediately elevated to the mayor's office. The corrupt supervisors then resigned to make way for a "clean" group.

Serene, indifferent to fate,
She sits beside the Golden Gate.

Bret Harte wrote this of San Francisco in the depressing days following the quake of 1868.

In 1906, the lines were recalled and published again and again in reference to the newly stricken City. Perhaps San Francisco could have been properly called "serene" in the few days of indirection that followed the fire, but not in the months and years to come later. Though many adjectives would describe the City, "serene" wouldn't have been among them. The City fairly

Add a bridge across the Bay and a tower to the top of Telegraph Hill, and you'll find the scene didn't change much between 1912, when this shot was taken, and today. Building at the corner of Vallejo and Taylor, lower right, is the "House of the Flag." (California Historical Society)

One day, when no one noticed, San Francisco was whole again. The streets bustled with normal traffic, and the noise of carpenters and riveters faded beneath the clamor of streetcars and news boys. Here, San Franciscans from every cut of life pass the corner of Kearny and Market on a foggy afternoon, not too unlike the crowds that thronged the streets on an April morning six years before. (California Historical Society)

burst with vitality once a little of the debris had been cleared away.

If you cut one of California's beloved native redwoods or one of the stately immigrant eucalyptus to the ground, you haven't killed a tree. In the great root system beneath the soil lies a storehouse of energy and sustenance that will send up new growth like a bolt. This was the story of San Francisco. From the ashes, the new City sprang in the image of the old. Grander, broader, more beautiful than ever—forever a joy to those who love her.

181

EPILOGUE: SMALL SCARS AND MEMORIES

The phoenix, an Egyptian symbol of immortality, rises from the ashes on San Francisco's seal. The mythological bird was incorporated into the design after disastrous fires of the early 1850s.

Montgomery Street from Telegraph Hill. (California Historical Society)

The Panama-Pacific International Exposition was built at Harbor View adjoining the Presidio after San Francisco won congressional approval to hold the fair. There had been stiff competition with other cities, particularly New Orleans, for the honor. (California Historical Society)

SAN FRANCISCO held open house in 1915. The Panama-Pacific International Exposition was an invitation to the world to come and see the City for which it had wept a short nine years before. It was an impressive affair—heavy with opulent architecture and sanguine art. Officially, the fair was held to celebrate the building of the Panama Canal. San Franciscans, however, frankly took greater pride and pleasure in the City's rebuilding than in the "Big Ditch."

The exposition was originally proposed in 1904, and preparations went ahead until the big fire put a dent in the plans. Some thought it would take ten, perhaps twenty or more, years to rebuild the town, and that the fair would have to be forgotten. But in December of 1906, a committee met in the temporary St. Francis Hotel—a rustic shed on Union Square—and the Pacific Ocean Exposition Company was formed. The planners faced many difficulties, but even World War I couldn't delay the celebration.

Today, Bernard Maybeck's Palace of Fine Arts stands in tranquil, decaying splendor—all that is left of the three-hundred-acre wonderland.

184

Jimmy Rolph, one of San Francisco's most popular mayors, took a back seat as one of his aides handled the pair of handsome grays pulling the last horsecar up Market. The Gaslight Era was dead, and the Age of Speed was on its way. (California Historical Society)

While the Exposition has faded in San Francisco's memory, many reminders and survivors of the earthquake and fire live on:

• The "Portals of the Past" sit timelessly on little Lloyd Lake in Golden Gate Park.

• If you look, you can find cracks in the terrazzo floor of the main Post Office that date back to the fateful morning.

• The Fairmont and St. Francis, the old mint and the Ferry Building, the Flood Building and the Merchant's Exchange are still with us, and all look as though they'll be around for the next big shake.

• Southhampton Shoals Lighthouse in northern San Francisco Bay sits firmly on piles that were tilted eleven degrees off vertical during the quake and never righted.

• At the foot of Sansome Street stands one of the ancient, iron-shuttered brick warehouses that survived in the shadow of Telegraph Hill.

• The two-hundred-mile earth rupture has healed on the surface, but the scar is there to see for all who care to look.

185

The face of old St. Mary's looked down upon a shabby house of pleasure before the fire, with an ageless admonition from Ecclesiastes, "Son, observe the time and fly from evil." Today, Bufano's statue of Sun Yat Sen looks out over the greenery of St. Mary's Square, where the brothel once stood. (San Francisco Chamber of Commerce)

San Francisco, September 1, 1907.

The Rabbi, the President and the Board of Directors of the Congregation Emanu El

to the Pastor, the Chairman and the Board of Directors of The First Unitarian Church.

Gentlemen

On the eve of the reconsecration of our House of worship our hearts turn with grateful sentiments towards you, whose generous hospitality, in a period of trouble and disorganization, enabled us to preserve and maintain our identity as a congregation of worshippers of the living God.

We will never forget your kindness and fraternal consideration. In your benevolent attitude toward us we recognize the spirit of fellowship in God, our common Father, and we, too, will treasure this spirit and acquaint our descendants with the great fact that—in the midst of the ruins of a great City—Jew and Christian, like men and brethren, worshipped God beneath the same roof.

May that same spirit of God and godliness lead you to the continuous accomplishment of His will on earth, that Love and Fellowship in Him may be manifested unto all men in our community.

And thus we part from you, and send you this token of our sincere, and most grateful acknowledgements.

For the Congregation Emanu El

Jacob Voorsanger, Rabbi   *I. C. Waugenheim, President*

Lillie Hitchcock Coit, celebrated darling of the volunteer firemen, gave this statue in remembrance of their dashing and often heroic work. The tower on top of Telegraph Hill in the background is another of her gifts to the City. (Paul Chaumont)

Almost twenty years before the fire, Congregation Emanu El opened the doors of their Sutter Street synagogue to the people of the First Unitarian Church. The Unitarians were without a place of worship, having relinquished their downtown church while the present one was under construction. The friendship grew over the years, and when fire gutted the temple in 1906, the Unitarians were able to return the gracious offer. For more than a year, the Jewish worshipers gathered at the church while their synagogue was rebuilt. To this day, the congregations meet for joint services once a year—on Thanksgiving Day.

- Hip-roofed frame houses can be found scattered across the hills of San Francisco that began life humbly in the fall of 1906 as "refugee shacks." Painted and landscaped and "built-onto" for five decades, they are sometimes hard to spot.
- Fort Ross and Mission San Juan Bautista carry on, completely repaired, as State Historical Monuments.
- Out at Sutro Baths, near the Cliff House, at least half the ten-cent stereoscopic machines show earthquake and fire scenes.
- Rows of "carpenter's gothic" houses stretch west from Van Ness where the fire never reached. But their ranks are thinning as the years go on.
- Cable cars still "twitch and rattle" over Nob Hill.

And that is just a sample. More than landmarks, though, San Francisco has memories.

Clubs have formed which meet to remember the day, and the newspapers never forget when April 18 rolls around.

Each year, the Late Watch—originally made up of the journalists who covered the big story—holds a banquet at the Press Club.

The "1906 Club" gathers for lunch at the Whitcomb Hotel.

And early in the morning of the eighteenth the South of Market Boys gather at Lotta's Fountain to place a wreath in memory of those who died South of the Slot so many years ago.

Although more than fifty years have passed since the German insurance companies turned their backs on

186

San Francisco, one San Franciscan is still trying to collect. His name is Edward F. Braunschweiger III. When the fire swept through the wholesale district, warehouses of a liquor business set up by his pioneer grandfather in 1859 went up in smoke. The Rhine and Moselle Fire Insurance Company withdrew, owing the Braunschweiger family $38,000, and the rest of San Francisco $4½ million more. Mr. Braunschweiger, as his mother before him, has spent many years seeking restitution. Since 1950, Congress and the Federal courts have heard his plea that the welching insurance company operated at the sufferance of the American Government, and that German funds from the Alien Property Custodian's office should be used to reimburse his parent's estate. With interest and other charges, his claim now totals more than $700,000.

Aften ten years of struggle, Mr. Braunschweiger is tiring a bit. It has been a losing battle, but you can be sure that as long as he has the energy, Congress, the courts, and our Presidents will continue to receive his highly-styled petitions and briefs until he wins. Here is a sample from the Congressional Record of 1955, in which he asks the late Senator Walter George to delay the German Peace Treaty until his claim is met. He

Huntington Park's neat geometry breaks the brick and concrete, stone and asphalt face of Nob Hill. The old Flood mansion, now the Pacific Union Club, squats indifferently across from the Fairmont, left, and Mark Hopkins, center. The Call Building, now the Central Tower, is not visible in this shot, but if you look carefully, you can find another 1906 landmark—the Whittell Building. (San Francisco Chamber of Commerce)

Chief Rudy Schubert, a member of 38 Engine in 1906, is pictured 50 years later beside one of the old pumpers (San Francisco News)

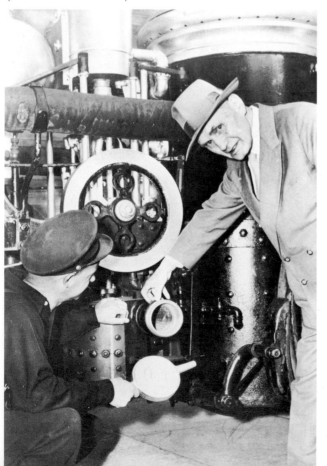

No great monument has been erected to commemorate the 1906 fire, but unmarked and half forgotten, the Portals of the Past have remained through the decades as a tranquil reminder. (Robert Cowgill)

South of Market Boys chat after placing memorial wreath on Lottie's Pump, as Lotta's Fountain was called by the irreverent, at 5:12 A.M. on a chilly morning—April 18, 1958. Palace Hotel, Monadnock Building, in background. (Dagmar Johnson)

Locked by the Bay and the Ocean, San Francisco's lovely profile has changed little since Gold Rush. (San Francisco Chamber of Commerce)

begins with a swipe at Senator Alexander Wiley, who failed to answer a previous request for help:

. . . Mr. Wiley . . . refused to answer my epistle . . . Non 'ob-stan'te, it is quite obvious and patent that someone is not up to *taw*, way below the *plimsoll's* line, a *chameleon* like person, and maybe a political Janus. I will let you sir, be the Judge.

Succinctly and laconically, the nib, the crux and the nub of my writing to you Senator, as Chairman of the Foreign Relations Committee, is that you now have before your august body a proposed Treaty with the neo Facto west German Nation. Now, as an American Citizen I must oppose favorable action on this Treaty and please record my protest officially in your minutes and send me a copy. You believe in the sanctity of property, do you not Senator, the bulwark of our American Democracy and before any such Treaty and/or Treaties as now proposed to your committee by the Department of State can or should be ratified, my claim *must* be adjudicated. . . .

Now in L'envoi, I may not agree with your committee's decision, but, sir, I will defend to the death, your committee's right to form its own opinion. With apologies for this last expiation, to an eminent Scholar and Philosopher, Jean Francois Marie Arouet.

I assign Senator George, Respectfully and Sincerely,

EDWARD F. BRAUNSCHWEIGER III

Everyone who knows Eddie, as his friends call him, hopes he wins the case. But no matter what the outcome, the dear man should be remembered by all who love San Francisco and the independent souls who punctuate her story with passion and whimsey.

One of the deepest marks left on the city is to be found in the Fire Department and the system which evolved from the lesson of 1906. Independent, multimillion-gallon reservoirs were established, cisterns were restored and built all through the concentrated areas, two salt-water pumping stations—one at Fort Mason and the other at Second and Townsend—were created and are maintained today on a round-the-clock schedule. "The City That Knows How," as President Taft called her, learned the hard way. May she never be tried again.

When the fiftieth anniversary arrived, San Francisco staged a five-day "Festival of Progress." It began at 5:13 on the morning of Wednesday, April 18, 1956, when the South of Market Boys met and placed their

Sparkling morning light reflects off Nob Hill in this crisp view from Telegraph Hill. (San Francisco Chamber of Commerce)

customary wreath at Lotta's Fountain, and it ended with a grand parade on Sunday, the twenty-second. Four hundred watched the placing of the wreath and 150,000 watched the parade as it coursed its way from the Ferry Building to the City Hall.

1957 was a lively year for earthquake *aficianados*. The city had just gone through the sharpest quake since the big one, and old-timers were happy to make copy for the anniversary editions. At the meeting of the 1906 Club, for instance, one of the survivors was asked by a reporter to compare the earthquakes. The old man inquired,

"What quake are you talking about, son?"

"The last one, sir, on March 22nd. How do you think it compares with the one in 1906?"

"My boy, the only other quake I would compare the 1906 one with is the one they had in 1892 and even that was just a conversation piece."

Part of the tradition, and perhaps the least desirable of all its elements, are the exaggerated stories of butchery and inhumanity. Stories grow, and facts begin to drift out of focus as the years pass. In 1956, one of the San Francisco dailies printed the following in a lead story of their anniversary edition:

"Fourteen men were shot, picked off like birds, trying to loot the United States Mint. Fourteen soldiers, caught by other soldiers in the act of looting a saloon, were hanged."

The story might have been taken from one of the hundred hasty, maudlin paperbacks that flooded the country after the fire and are now being shunted into the locked cages of our libraries as rare books. But none of it is true, even remotely.

Let us hope that innocent repetition of such stories will not establish them as the "truth" of one of mankind's greatest trials. Pain and death were part of it, to be sure, but beastiality was absent.

San Francisco, and mankind for that matter, can look back to 1906 with pride, for tenderness, not brutality, prevailed.

Years later, the late Judge Isadore L. "Ike" Harris summed it for his generation, and for ours and for those to come when he recalled . . . "a brotherhood of man such as I wish could come without tragedy."

INDEX